Lebanon American iron and steel manufacturing co

American Iron and Steel Manufacturing Company

Lebanon American iron and steel manufacturing co

American Iron and Steel Manufacturing Company

ISBN/EAN: 9783743311060

Manufactured in Europe, USA, Canada, Australia, Japa

Cover: Foto ©Suzi / pixelio.de

Manufactured and distributed by brebook publishing software
(www.brebook.com)

Lebanon American iron and steel manufacturing co

American Iron and Steel Manufacturing Company

INCORPORATED 1899

American Iron and Steel Manufacturing Company

GENERAL OFFICE

LEBANON, PENNA., U. S. A.

MANUFACTURERS OF

Refined Merchant Bar Iron,

Bolts, Nuts, Washers, Boiler, Tank, Bridge and Ship Rivets, Lag Screws, Turnbuckles, Harvey Patent Grip Thread Track Bolts, Soft Steel Bolts with Cold-pressed Threads, Railroad Spikes,

Arch Bars, Body Bolsters and other Car Forgings,

Rods and Irons for Bridges and Buildings, etc.

Mills and Factories Located at

READING, ⎫
LEBANON, ⎭ PENNSYLVANIA, U. S. A.

On September 1, 1899, this Company purchased the works and business of the Pennsylvania Bolt and Nut Company, Lebanon Iron Company and East Lebanon Iron Company, all of Lebanon, Pennsylvania, and J. H. Sternbergh & Son and the National Bolt, Nut & Rivet Works, of Reading, Pennsylvania. These plants were among the largest and best of their kind not merely in the United States, but anywhere in the world, with an established reputation in the field each occupied.

The consolidation of the various interests mentioned makes the American Iron and Steel Manufacturing Company the largest manufacturers of bolts, nuts, rivets and kindred articles on the globe. Our new Company employs 4,000 men, and in the department of finished bar iron and steel alone the annual product will be about 150,000 tons. In addition to this large output of bars, our various plants make, on a large scale, all kinds of Car Forgings, Steam Railroad and Traction Forgings, Ship Yard Supplies, Ship Chandlery Supplies, Railroad Spikes, Turnbuckles, Washers, etc. It will be our aim to provide ourselves at all times with the most modern machinery, and maintain a high standard for excellence of material and workmanship.

We carry in stock a large quantity of finished goods, and are able to execute orders with promptness. We pay as close attention to small orders as we do to large ones.

We invite the confidence of buyers.

American Iron and Steel Manufacturing Co.

Lebanon, Pa., November 1, 1899

TERMS

Unless otherwise specified or agreed upon, all bills are sold for Cash, and are payable within thirty days from date of invoice, without discount or rebate.

For accounts not paid at maturity we will draw at sight, after giving notice of our intention.

It is understood that our quotations are made for immediate acceptance, and are subject to change without notice.

All goods are delivered free on board cars at our works, unless otherwise specified. When any freight allowance is quoted, it is understood that it is not applicable to quantities less than three hundred pounds.

Claims for errors and omissions must be made within five days after receipt of goods.

Manufacturers' Standard List of

Machine Bolts.

With Square Heads and Square Nuts.
Finished Points.—Price per Hundred.

Adopted September 20, 1899, to take effect October 1, 1899.

Fig. 1.   Fig. 2.

Length Inches	¼	5/16	⅜	7/16	½	9/16 & ⅝	¾	⅞	1	1⅛	1¼
1½	1.70	2.00	2.40	2.80	3.60	5.20	7.20	10.50	15.10	22.50	30.00
2	1.78	2.12	2.56	3.00	3.86	5.58	7.70	11.20	16.00	23.70	31.50
2½	1.86	2.24	2.72	3.20	4.12	5.96	8.20	11.90	16.90	24.90	33.00
3	1.94	2.36	2.88	3.40	4.38	6.34	8.70	12.60	17.80	26.10	34.50
3½	2.02	2.48	3.04	3.60	4.64	6.72	9.20	13.30	18.70	27.30	36.00
4	2.10	2.60	3.20	3.80	4.90	7.10	9.70	14.00	19.60	28.50	37.50
4½	2.18	2.72	3.36	4.00	5.16	7.48	10.20	14.70	20.50	29.70	39.00
5	2.26	2.84	3.52	4.20	5.42	7.86	10.70	15.40	21.40	30.90	40.50
5½	2.34	2.96	3.68	4.40	5.68	8.24	11.20	16.10	22.30	32.10	42.00
6	2.42	3.08	3.84	4.60	5.94	8.62	11.70	16.80	23.20	33.30	43.50
6½	2.50	3.20	4.00	4.80	6.20	9.00	12.20	17.50	24.10	34.50	45.00
7	2.58	3.32	4.16	5.00	6.46	9.38	12.70	18.20	25.00	35.70	46.50
7½	2.66	3.44	4.32	5.20	6.72	9.76	13.20	18.90	25.90	36.90	48.00
8	2.74	3.56	4.48	5.40	6.98	10.14	13.70	19.60	26.80	38.10	49.50
9	2.90	3.80	4.80	5.80	7.50	10.90	14.70	21.00	28.60	40.50	52.50
10	3.06	4.04	5.12	6.20	8.02	11.66	15.70	22.40	30.40	42.90	55.50
11	3.22	4.28	5.44	6.60	8.54	12.42	16.70	23.80	32.20	45.30	58.50
12	3.38	4.52	5.76	7.00	9.06	13.18	17.70	25.20	34.00	47.70	61.50
13	..	..	6.08	7.40	9.58	13.94	18.70	26.60	35.80	50.10	64.50
14	..	..	6.40	7.80	10.10	14.70	19.70	28.00	37.60	52.50	67.50
15	..	..	6.72	8.20	10.62	15.46	20.70	29.40	39.40	54.90	70.50
16	..	..	7.04	8.60	11.14	16.22	21.70	30.80	41.20	57.30	73.50
17					11.66	16.98	22.70	32.20	43.00	59.70	76.50
18					12.18	17.74	23.70	33.60	44.80	62.10	79.50
19					12.70	18.50	24.70	35.00	46.60	64.50	82.50
20					13.22	19.26	25.70	36.40	48.40	66.90	85.50
21							26.70	37.80	50.20	69.30	88.50
22							27.70	39.20	52.00	71.70	91.50
23							28.70	40.60	53.80	74.10	94.50
24							29.70	42.00	55.60	76.50	97.50
25							30.70	43.40	57.40	78.90	100.50
26							31.70	44.80	59.20	81.30	103.50
27							32.70	46.20	61.00	83.70	106.50
28							33.70	47.60	62.80	86.10	109.50
29							34.70	49.00	64.60	88.50	112.50
30							35.70	50.40	66.40	90.90	115.50

These list prices apply only on lots of not less than 100 of a size.
Unless otherwise specified we will send all Machine Bolts with square heads and hot pressed square nuts.

The following extras are a part of the Machine Bolt list:

Bolts with Hexagon Heads or Hexagon Nuts, 10 per cent. extra.

With both Hexagon Heads and Hexagon Nuts, 20 per cent. extra.

Joint Bolts with Oblong Nuts, and Bolts with Tee Heads, 10 per cent. extra.

Bolts requiring extra upsets to form the head, and other Special Bolts with irregular threads and unusual dimensions of heads or nuts will be charged extra at our discretion.

All Bolts are cut U. S. S. Thread unless ordered otherwise. Special Threads at advanced prices.

Weight of Machine Bolts, see pages 8 and 9.

For dimensions of bolt heads and nuts see page 56.

We make Brass, Tobin Bronze and Galvanized Bolts and Nuts, and will quote prices on receipt of specifications.

In ordering Bolts please specify length from under head to point, except for countersunk head bolts, which are measured over all. Name the diameter first and then the length, thus: ½×3; also state whether hot pressed or C. and T. nuts are wanted.

Manufacturers' Standard List of

Net Prices for Extra Length of Threads and Extra Nuts.

Adopted September 20, 1899, to take effect October 1, 1899.

Size of Bolt	1/4	5/16	3/8	7/16	1/2	9/16 & 5/8	3/4	7/8	1
Extreme Length of Thread in inches	3/4	15/16	1 1/8	1 5/16	1 1/2	1 7/8	2 1/4	2 5/8	3
For each additional 1/4" of Thread, per 100 Bolts	.02	.02	.02½	.03	.04	.06	.08	.10	.12
For one extra Square Nut, per 100 Bolts	.25	.35	.45	.55	.65	.85	1.35	2.00	3.00
For one extra Hexagon Nut, per 100 Bolts	.35	.45	.55	.70	.85	1.15	1.75	2.50	3.60

Soft Steel Machine Bolts.

With Cold Pressed Threads, Square Heads and Nuts. Finished Points.

List prices for these Bolts same as given on page 6.

Please observe that the thread is not cut in the usual manner, but is raised slightly above the surface of the shank by cold pressure, thus preserving the full strength of the Bolt in the threaded portion. They are about fifty per cent. stronger than ordinary iron cut Thread Bolts and will break in the shank rather than the threaded part, under tensile strain.

Fig. 3.

Button Head Square Neck Bolt.

Special Prices on application.

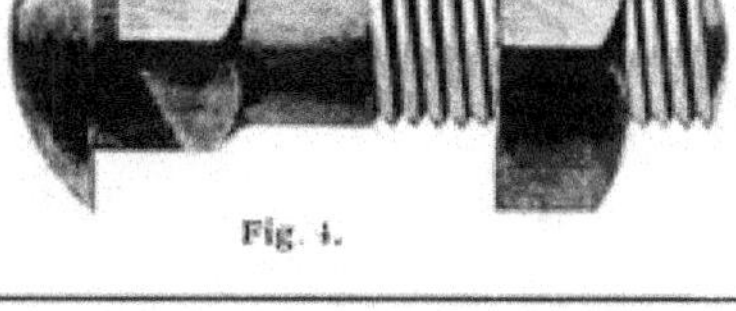

Fig. 4.

Average Weight per 100 of Machine Bolts.

Square Heads and Square Nuts.

Diam.	$\frac{1}{4}$	$\frac{5}{16}$	$\frac{3}{8}$	$\frac{7}{16}$	$\frac{1}{2}$	$\frac{9}{16}$	$\frac{5}{8}$	$\frac{3}{4}$	$\frac{7}{8}$	1
Length	lbs.	lbs.	lbs.	lbs.	lbs.	lbs.	lbs.	lbs.	lbs.	lbs.
1½ in.	3.9	6.2	9.7	14.7	20.4	26.0	37.0	58.0	..	..
2 "	4.6	7.2	11.3	16.5	22.4	29 0	39.9	63.2	97.7	145
2½ "	5.4	8.2	12.9	18.5	25.0	32.2	44.1	69.0	105.6	153
3 "	6.2	9.3	14.5	20.5	27.8	35.4	48.3	75.2	113.8	163
3½ "	6.9	10.4	16.1	22.6	30.6	38.7	52.5	81.4	122.0	174
4 "	7.6	11.5	17.7	24.7	33.4	42.0	56.7	87.6	130.2	185
4½ "	8.3	12.6	19.2	26.8	36.2	45.3	60.9	93.8	138.4	196
5 "	9.0	13.7	20.7	28.9	39.0	48.6	65.1	100.0	146.6	207
5½ "	9.7	14.8	22.2	31.0	41.8	51.9	69.2	106.1	154.9	218
6 "	10.4	15.9	23.7	33.1	44.6	55.2	73.4	112.2	163.2	229
6½ "	11.1	17.0	25.2	35.2	47.4	58.5	77.6	118.3	171.5	240
7 "	11.8	18.1	26.7	37.3	50.2	61.8	81.8	124.4	179.8	251
7½ "	12.5	19.2	28.2	39.4	53.1	65.1	86.0	130.5	187.1	262
8 "	13.2	20.3	29.7	41.5	56.0	68.5	90.0	136.6	195.4	273
9 "			33.1	45.7	61.5	75.2	98.0	148.8	212.0	295
10 "			36.5	49.9	67.0	81.9	106.3	161.0	229.0	317
11 "			40.0	54.1	72.5	88.7	114.6	173.2	246.0	339
12 "			43.5	58.3	78.0	95.5	122.9	184.4	263.0	361
13 "					83.5	102.3	131.2	196.6	280.0	383
14 "			..	..	89.0	109.1	139.5	208.8	297.0	405
15 "					94.5	116.0	148.0	221.0	314.0	427
16 "					100.0	123.0	156.5	233.2	331.0	449
17 "					105.5	130.0	165.0	245.4	348.0	471
18 "			..	..	111.0	137.0	173.5	257.6	365.0	493
19 "					116.5	144.0	182.0	269.8	382.0	515
20 "					122.0	151.0	190.5	282.0	399.0	537
21 "			..	..	..	..	198.0	294.0	416.0	559
22 "					..	..	206.0	306.0	437.0	581
23 "						..	215.0	318.0	454.0	603
24 "							224.0	330.0	470.0	625

Average Weight per 100 of Machine Bolts.

Square Heads and Square Nuts.

Length	1⅛ inch Diameter	1¼ inch Diameter	1⅜ inch Diameter	1½ inch Diameter	1¾ inch Diameter	2 inch Diameter
3 inch	240 lbs.	309 lbs.	350 lbs.	480 lbs.	. . .	. . .
3½ "	253 "	325 "	370 "	500 "	. . .	. .
4 "	267 "	342 "	390 "	520 "	800 lbs.	. . .
4½ "	281 "	359 "	410 "	545 "	833 "	. . .
5 "	295 "	376 "	430 "	570 "	866 "	1370 lbs.
5½ "	309 "	394 "	450 "	595 "	900 "	1414 "
6 "	323 "	412 "	470 "	620 "	934 "	1458 "
6½ "	337 "	430 "	490 "	645 "	968 "	1502 "
7 "	351 "	448 "	510 "	670 "	1002 "	1546 "
7½ "	365 "	466 "	530 "	695 "	1036 "	1590 "
8 "	379 "	484 "	550 "	725 "	1070 "	1634 "
9 "	407 "	518 "	590 "	775 "	1138 "	1722 "
10 "	435 "	552 "	630 "	825 "	1206 "	1810 "
11 "	463 "	586 "	670 "	875 "	1274 "	1898 "
12 "	491 "	620 "	710 "	925 "	1342 "	1986 "
13 "	519 "	655 "	751 "	975 "	1410 "	2074 "
14 "	547 "	690 "	793 "	1025 "	1478 "	2162 "
15 "	575 "	725 "	835 "	1075 "	1548 "	2250 "
16 "	603 "	760 "	877 "	1125 "	1616 "	2338 "
17 "	931 "	795 "	919 "	1175 "	1684 "	2426 "
18 "	659 "	830 "	961 "	1225 "	1752 "	2514 "
19 "	687 "	865 "	1003 "	1275 "	1820 "	2602 "
20 "	715 "	900 "	1045 "	1325 "	1888 "	2690 "
21 "	743 "	935 "	1087 "	1375 "	1956 "	2778 "
22 "	771 "	970 "	1129 "	1425 "	2024 "	2866 "
23 "	799 "	1005 "	1171 "	1475 "	2092 "	2954 "
24 "	827 "	1040 "	1213 "	1525 "	2160 "	3042 "
25 "	855 "	1075 "	1255 "	1575 "	2228 "	3130 "

Manufacturers' Standard List of

Blank Bolts.

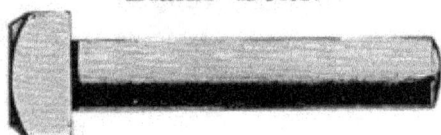

Fig. 5.

With either Square or Round Heads. Finished Points. Price per Hundred.

Adopted January 30, 1895, to take effect February 14, 1895.

Length in Inches	¼	⁵⁄₁₆	⅜	⁷⁄₁₆	½	⁹⁄₁₆ & ⅝	¾	⅞	1
1½	1.20	1.40	1.60	2.00	2.50	4.00	5.60	7.80	10.40
2	1.30	1.52	1.74	2.18	2.74	4.36	6.10	8.50	11.30
2½	1.40	1.64	1.88	2.36	2.98	4.72	6.60	9.20	12.20
3	1.50	1.76	2.02	2.54	3.22	5.08	7.10	9.90	13.10
3½	1.60	1.88	2.16	2.72	3.46	5.44	7.60	10.60	14.00
4	1.70	2.00	2.30	2.90	3.70	5.80	8.10	11.30	14.90
4½	1.80	2.12	2.44	3.08	3.94	6.16	8.60	12.00	15.80
5	1.90	2.24	2.58	3.26	4.18	6.52	9.10	12.70	16.70
5½	2.00	2.36	2.72	3.44	4.42	6.88	9.60	13.40	17.60
6	2.10	2.48	2.86	3.62	4.66	7.24	10.10	14.10	18.50
6½	2.20	2.60	3.00	3.80	4.90	7.60	10.60	14.80	19.40
7	2.30	2.72	3.14	3.98	5.14	7.96	11.10	15.50	20.30
7½	2.40	2.84	3.28	4.16	5.38	8.32	11.60	16.20	21.20
8	2.50	2.96	3.42	4.34	5.62	8.68	12.10	16.90	22.10
9	2.70	3.20	3.70	4.70	6.10	9.40	13.10	18.30	23.90
10	2.90	3.44	3.98	5.06	6.58	10.12	14.10	19.70	25.70
11	3.10	3.68	4.26	5.42	7.06	10.84	15.10	21.10	27.50
12	3.30	3.92	4.54	5.78	7.54	11.56	16.10	22.50	29.30
13	. .	. .	4.82	6.14	8.02	12.28	17.10	23.90	31.10
14	. .	. .	5.10	6.50	8.50	13.00	18.10	25.30	32.90
15	. .	. .	5.38	6.86	8.98	13.72	19.10	26.70	34.70
16	. .	. .	5.66	7.22	9.46	14.44	20.10	28.10	36.50
17	. .	. .	. .	. .	9.94	15.16	21.10	29.50	38.30
18	. .	. .	.	. .	10.42	15.88	22.10	30.90	40.10
19	. .	. .	. .	. .	10.90	16.60	23.10	32.30	41.90
20	. .	. .	. .	. .	11.38	17.32	24.10	33.70	43.70

The following extras are a part of this list :

Blank Bolts with Hexagon Heads or Tee Heads, 10 per cent. extra.

Bolts requiring extra upsets to form the head will be charged extra at our discretion.

Weight of Square Head Blank Bolts.

Average Weight per Hundred.

Dia	$\frac{3}{8}$	$\frac{7}{16}$	$\frac{1}{2}$	$\frac{5}{8}$	$\frac{3}{4}$	$\frac{7}{8}$	1	$1\frac{1}{4}$	$1\frac{1}{4}$	$1\frac{1}{2}$
Length	lbs.	lbs.	lbs.	lbs.	lbs.	lbs.	lbs.	lbs	lbs.	lbs
$\frac{3}{4}$	5.6	8.7	11.2	.	.	. .	. .	. .	. .	. .
1	6.4	9.7	12.6	23.0	. .	. .	. .	. .	. .	. .
$1\frac{1}{4}$	7.2	10.7	14.0	24.9	39.5	. .	. .	. .	. .	. .
$1\frac{1}{2}$	8.0	11.7	15.4	27.1	42.5	63.0	. .	. .	. .	. .
$1\frac{3}{4}$	8.8	12.7	16.8	29.0	45.5	67.0	90	. .	. .	. .
2	9.6	13.7	18.2	31.0	48.5	71.0	95	. .	. .	. .
$2\frac{1}{4}$	10.4	14.7	19.6	33.0	51.5	75.2	100	141	. .	. .
$2\frac{1}{2}$	11.2	15.7	21.0	35.0	54.5	79.4	105	149	. .	. .
$2\frac{3}{4}$	12.0	16.7	22.4	37.0	57.5	83.7	110	157	. .	. .
3	12.8	17.7	23.8	39.0	60.5	88.0	115	165	215	370
$3\frac{1}{2}$	14.4	19.7	26.6	43.5	66.5	96.3	125	180	232	392
4	16.0	21.7	29.4	48.0	72.7	104.5	136	195	249	414
$4\frac{1}{2}$	17.5	23.7	31.2	52.5	78.9	112.8	147	210	266	437
5	19.0	25.7	35.0	56.5	85.1	121.0	158	225	283	461
$5\frac{1}{2}$	20.5	27.7	37.8	60.5	91.3	129.3	169	240	300	485
6	22.0	29.7	40.6	64.6	97.5	137.5	180	265	317	510
7	25.0	33.7	46.0	72.8	109.0	154.0	202	290	351	560
8	28.0	37.7	51.5	81.0	121.0	171.0	223	315	386	610
9	. .	41.7	56.7	89.0	133.0	188.0	245	340	420	660
10	. .	45.7	62.0	97.0	145.0	205.0	267	365	453	710
11	. .		67.5	105.0	157.0	222.0	288	390	488	760
12	. .	. .	73.0	114.0	170.0	239.0	310	415	523	810

Bolt Ends.

Fig. 6.

With Square Nuts.

Size of Iron	Length	Price per lb.	Size of Iron	Length	Price per lb.
$\frac{7}{16}$ inch	6 inch	.32	$1\frac{1}{8}$ inch	14 inch	.11
$\frac{1}{2}$ "	6 "	.25	$1\frac{1}{4}$ "	15 "	.11
$\frac{9}{16}$ "	6 "	.20	$1\frac{1}{2}$ "	16 "	.11
$\frac{5}{8}$ "	7 "	.18	$1\frac{5}{8}$ "	17 "	.12
$\frac{11}{16}$ "	7 "	.16	$1\frac{3}{4}$ "	18 "	.12
$\frac{1}{2}$ & $\frac{7}{16}$ "	8 "	.14	$1\frac{7}{8}$ "	19 "	.12
$\frac{5}{8}$ "	9 "	.12	2 "	20 "	.12
$\frac{3}{4}$ "	10 "	.10	$2\frac{1}{4}$ "	22 "	.14
$\frac{7}{8}$ "	11 "	.10	$2\frac{1}{2}$ "	24 "	.14
1 "	12 "	.10	$2\frac{3}{4}$ "	24 "	.16
$1\frac{1}{8}$ "	13 "	.10	3 "	26 "	.18

Please state on order whether Hot Pressed or Cold Punched C. and T. Nuts are to be furnished.   Hexagon Nuts, 10 per cent. extra.

Bolt Ends shorter than above Standard lengths, in lots of 100 and over, will be charged at the price per hundred of Machine Bolts of same length, subject to same discount ; in smaller lots extra.

Bolt Ends cut with left hand threads, or with Upset Ends, at special prices.

Weight of Bolt Ends.

With Square Nuts.

Average Weight per Hundred.

		$\frac{5}{8}\times 9$	84 lbs.	$1\frac{1}{8}\times 15$	865 lbs.	$2\ \times 20$	2400 lbs.
		$\frac{3}{4}\times 10$	145 "	$1\frac{1}{2}\times 16$	1075 "	$2\frac{1}{4}\times 22$	3150 "
$\frac{7}{16}\times 6$	14 lbs.	$\frac{7}{8}\times 11$	210 "	$1\frac{5}{8}\times 17$	1350 "	$2\frac{1}{2}\times 24$	4200 "
$\frac{3}{4}\times 7$	24 "	$1\ \times 12$	300 "	$1\frac{3}{4}\times 18$	1670 "	$2\frac{3}{4}\times 24$	5100 "
$\frac{7}{16}\times 7$	34 "	$1\frac{1}{8}\times 13$	445 "	$1\frac{7}{8}\times 19$	1900 "	$3\ \times 26$	6400 "
$\frac{1}{2}\times 8$	49 "	$1\frac{1}{4}\times 14$	644 "				

All Bolt Ends are fitted with U. S. Standard Nuts.

Hanger Bolts.

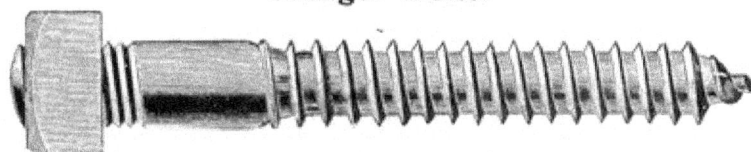

Fig. 7.

Price per Hundred—In 100 lots.

Length over all	3/8	1/2	5/8	3/4	7/8	1	1 1/8	1 1/4
3 in.	5.00	6.50						
4 "		7.00						
5 "		7.50	9.75					
6 "		8.00	10.50	13.50	16.50			
7 "		8.50	11.25	14.50	18.00	25.50		
8 "		9.00	12.00	15.50	19.50	27.00	36.00	
9 "			12.75	16.50	21.00	28.50	38.00	54.00
10 "			13.50	17.50	22.50	30.00	40.00	57.00
11 "				18.50	24.00	31.50	42.00	60.00
12 "				19.50	25.50	33.00	44.00	63.00
14 "				21.50	28.50	36.00	48.00	69.00
16 "					31.50	39.00	52.00	75.00
18 "						42.00	56.00	81.00

With Hexagon Nuts, 10 per cent. extra.

We are prepared to furnish Hanger Bolts with Gimlet Points, also with Iron Pipe Thread in place of U. S. Standard Thread on Nut End, at special prices.

Hanger Bolts.

With Hexagon Nuts.

Approximate Weight per Hundred.

Length	1/2	5/8	3/4	7/8	1	1 1/8	1 1/4	1 3/8	1 1/2
4 in.	23								
6 "	33	51	76	100					
8 "	43	65	93	132	165	245	285		
10 "		79	110	160	208	287	335	435	505
12 "			130	190	250	320	385	490	570
14 "				220	286	362	435	545	650
16 "						405	485	600	720

Manufacturers' Standard List of

Coach and Lag Screws.

Fig. 8.

With Square Heads.   Price per Hundred.

With Either Cone Points or Gimlet Points.

Adopted September 20, 1899, to take effect October 1, 1899.

Length in Inches	$\frac{5}{16}$	$\frac{3}{8}$	$\frac{7}{16}$	$\frac{1}{2}$	$\frac{9}{16}$ & $\frac{5}{8}$	$\frac{3}{4}$	$\frac{7}{8}$	1
1½	2.25	2.70	3.15	3.75	. .	. .	. .	. .
2	2.45	2.96	3.47	4.11	5.00	. .	. .	. .
2½	2.65	3.22	3.79	4.47	5.50	7.90	. .	. .
3	2.85	3.48	4.11	4.83	6.00	8.60	12.50	. .
3½	3.05	3.74	4.43	5.19	6.50	9.30	13.50	18.20
4	3.25	4.00	4.75	5.55	7.00	10.00	14.50	19.50
4½	3.45	4.26	5.07	5.91	7.50	10.70	15.50	20.80
5	3.65	4.52	5.39	6.27	8.00	11.40	16.50	22.10
5½	3.85	4.78	5.71	6.63	8.50	12.10	17.50	23.40
6	4.05	5.04	6.03	6.99	9.00	12.80	18.50	24.70
6½	. .	. .	6.35	7.35	9.50	13.50	19.50	26.00
7	. .	. .	6.67	7.71	10.00	14.20	20.50	27.30
7½	. .	. .	6.99	8.07	10.50	14.90	21.50	28.60
8	. .	. .	7.31	8.43	11.00	15.60	22.50	29.90
9	. .	. .	7.95	9.15	12.00	17.00	24.50	32.50
10	. .	. .	. .	9.87	13.00	18.40	26.50	35.10
11	. .	. .	. .	10.59	14.00	19.80	28.50	37.70
12	. .	. .	. .	11.31	15.00	21.20	30.50	40.30

The following extras are a part of the Coach and Lag Screw List :
Hexagon Heads 10 per cent. extra.
Skein Screws are sold at the same price as Lag Screws.
Fetter Drive Screws and Pole Steps black or galvanized, see page 40.
Ore Washery Screws, Fig. 111, at Special price.

Weight of Square Head Lag Screws.

Average Weight per Hundred.

Dia.	$\frac{5}{16}$	$\frac{3}{8}$	$\frac{7}{16}$	$\frac{1}{2}$	$\frac{9}{16}$	$\frac{5}{8}$	$\frac{3}{4}$	$\frac{7}{8}$	1	$1\frac{1}{8}$	$1\frac{1}{4}$	$1\frac{1}{2}$
Long	lbs.	lbs.	lbs.	lbs.	lbs.	lbs.	lbs.	lbs.	lbs.	lbs.	lbs.	lbs.
1½	4.2	6.5	9.2	13.0	..	..	..	..	..	..	..	..
1¾	4.7	7.1	10.0	13.8	..	..	..	..	..	..	..	..
2	5.2	7.7	10.9	14.9	23.0	24.8	..	..	..	..	..	..
2¼	5.7	8.4	11.8	16.1	24.5	27.3	..	..	..	..	..	..
2½	6.2	9.2	12.7	17.4	26.0	29.0	43.0	..	..	..	..	..
3	7.2	10.6	14.6	19.0	29.2	32.9	48.3	75.0	..	..	..	..
3½	8.2	12.0	16.6	21.5	32.5	36.9	53.8	78.5	90	..	..	..
4	9.2	13.5	18.8	24.0	35.9	41.0	59.6	82.0	99	..	..	..
4½	10.2	15.0	20.7	26.5	39.3	44.9	65.5	86.0	108	..	..	..
5	11.3	16.5	22.8	29.0	42.7	48.8	71.5	90.0	118	150	..	..
5½	12.4	18.0	24.9	31.5	46.1	52.7	77.5	98.0	128	163	..	..
6	13.5	19.5	27.0	34.0	49.5	56.6	83.5	106.0	138	176	240	..
7	..	..	31.1	39.0	56.3	64.5	95.5	122.5	158	208	270	..
8	..	..	35.2	44.0	63.1	72.5	107.6	139.0	178	230	300	420
9	..	..	..	49.0	69.9	80.5	119.8	155.5	198	257	332	468
10	..	..	.	54.0	76.7	88.5	131.0	172.0	219	284	365	516
11	..	..	.	..	83.5	96.5	143.1	188.5	240	311	395	564
12	..	..	..	..	90.5	104.5	155.4	205.0	261	338	425	612

Manufacturers' Standard List of

Common Carriage Bolts.

Fig. 9.

Price per Hundred.

Adopted January 30, 1895, to take effect February 14, 1895.

Length	¼	⁵⁄₁₆	⅜	⁷⁄₁₆	½	⁹⁄₁₆ & ⅝	¾
1½	1.00	1.20	. .	. .	. .	. .	. .
1¾	1.04	1.25	. .	. .	. .	. .	. .
2	1.08	1.30	1.50	2.20	. .	. .	. .
2¼	1.12	1.35	1.57	2.28	. .	. .	. .
2½	1.16	1.40	1.64	2.36	. .	. .	. .
2¾	1.20	1.45	1.71	2.44	. .	. .	. .
3	1.24	1.50	1.78	2.52	3.00	5.00	7.20
3¼	1.28	1.55	1.85	2.60	3.10	5.15	7.40
3½	1.32	1.60	1.92	2.68	3.20	5.30	7.60
3¾	1.36	1.65	1.99	2.76	3.30	5.45	7.80
4	1.40	1.70	2.06	2.84	3.40	5.60	8.00
4¼	1.44	1.75	2.13	2.92	3.50	5.75	8.20
4½	1.48	1.80	2.20	3.00	3.60	5.90	8.40
4¾	1.52	1.85	2.27	3.08	3.70	6.05	8.60
5	1.56	1.90	2.34	3.16	3.80	6.20	8.80
5½	1.64	2.00	2.48	3.32	4.00	6.50	9.20
6	1.72	2.10	2.62	3.48	4.20	6.80	9.60
6½	1.80	2.20	2.76	3.64	4.40	7.10	10.00
7	1.88	2.30	2.90	3.80	4.60	7.40	10.40
7½	1.96	2.40	3.04	3.96	4.80	7.70	10.80
8	2.04	2.50	3.18	4.12	5.00	8.00	11.20
8½	2.12	2.60	3.32	4.28	5.20	8.30	11.60
9	2.20	2.70	3.46	4.44	5.40	8.60	12.00
9½	2.28	2.80	3.60	4.60	5.60	8.90	12.40
10	2.36	2.90	3.74	4.76	5.80	9.20	12.80
11	2.52	3.10	4.02	5.08	6.20	9.80	13.60
12	2.68	3.30	4.30	5.40	6.60	10.40	14.40
13	2.84	3.50	4.58	5.72	7.00	11.00	15.20
14	3.00	3.70	4.86	6.04	7.40	11.60	16.00
15	3.16	3.90	5.14	6.36	7.80	12.20	16.80
16	3.32	4.10	5.42	6.68	8.20	12.80	17.60
17	3.48	4.30	5.70	7.00	8.60	13.40	18.40
18	3.64	4.50	5.98	7.32	9.00	14.00	19.20
19	3.80	4.70	6.26	7.64	9.40	14.60	20.00
20	3.96	4.90	6.54	7.96	9.80	15.20	20.80

Extra for extra length of threads and extra nuts, same as on Machine Bolts,
see page 7.

Weight of Common Carriage Bolts.

Table showing the average weight in pounds of 100 Common Carriage Bolts of sizes enumerated.

Length	$\frac{1}{4}$	$\frac{5}{16}$	$\frac{3}{8}$	$\frac{7}{16}$	$\frac{1}{2}$	$\frac{5}{8}$
1	2.8	4.8	6.9	9.4	14.5	28.0
1 $\frac{1}{4}$	3.1	5.2	7.6	10.4	15.9	30.0
1 $\frac{1}{2}$	3.4	5.7	8.3	11.4	17.3	32.0
1 $\frac{3}{4}$	3.7	6.1	9.0	12.4	18.6	34.0
2	4.0	6.6	9.7	13.3	20.0	36.0
2 $\frac{1}{4}$	4.4	7.0	10.4	14.3	21.4	38.0
2 $\frac{1}{2}$	4.7	7.5	11.1	15.3	22.8	40.0
2 $\frac{3}{4}$	5.0	7.9	11.8	16.3	24.2	42.0
3	5.3	8.4	12.5	17.3	25.5	44.0
3 $\frac{1}{2}$	5.9	9.3	13.9	19.3	28.3	48.0
4	6.6	10.2	15.3	21.3	31.0	52.0
4 $\frac{1}{2}$	7.2	11.1	16.7	23.3	33.8	56.0
5	7.8	12.0	18 0	25.3	36.5	60.0
5 $\frac{1}{2}$	8.4	12.9	19.4	27.3	39.3	64.0
6	9.0	13.8	20.8	29.3	42.0	68.0
6 $\frac{1}{2}$	9.7	14.7	21.2	31.2	44.8	72.0
7	10.3	15.6	23.6	33.2	47.5	76.0
7 $\frac{1}{2}$	10.9	16.5	25.0	35.2	50.3	80.0
8	11.6	17.4	26.4	37.2	53.0	84.0
8 $\frac{1}{2}$	. .	18.4	27.8	39.2	55.8	88.0
9	. .	19.3	29.2	41.2	58.5	92.0
9 $\frac{1}{2}$	. .	20.2	30.6	43.1	61.3	96.0
10	. .	21.0	32.0	45.1	64.0	100.0
10 $\frac{1}{2}$	. .	. .	33.4	47.1	66.8	104.0
11	. .	. .	34.8	49.1	69.5	108.0
11 $\frac{1}{2}$	. .	. .	36.2	51.0	72.3	112.0
12	. .	. .	37.5	53.0	75.0	116.0

Manufacturers' Standard List of

Plow Bolts,

Either Iron or Steel.

Fig. 10.　　　　Fig. 11.　　　　Fig. 12.　　　　Fig. 13.

Price per Hundred.—With Right or Left Hand Threads as may be ordered.

Length	$\frac{5}{16}$	$\frac{3}{8}$	$\frac{7}{16}$	$\frac{1}{2}$	$\frac{9}{16}$	$\frac{5}{8}$
1¼	1.70	2.00	2.60	3.50	4.50	5.70
1½	1.80	2.10	2.75	3.70	4.75	6.00
1¾	1.90	2.20	2.90	3.90	5.00	6.30
2	2.00	2.30	3.05	4.10	5.25	6.60
2¼	2.10	2.40	3.20	4.30	5.50	6.90
2½	2.20	2.50	3.35	4.50	5.75	7.20
2¾	2.30	2.60	3.50	4.70	6.00	7.50
3	2.40	2.70	3.65	4.90	6.25	7.80
3¼	2.50	2.80	3.80	5.10	6.50	8.10
3½	2.60	2.90	3.95	5.30	6.75	8.40
3¾	2.70	3.00	4.10	5.50	7.00	8.70
4	2.80	3.10	4.25	5.70	7.25	9.00

Hexagon Nuts, 10 per cent. extra.
Special Heads charged at an extra price at our discretion.
In ordering Plow Bolts please specify the figure number, to enable us to make the heads exactly as required.　The length of Plow Bolts is measured over all.
Unless otherwise ordered, we will make all countersunk heads at an angle of thirty-five degrees.
These Bolts can be furnished either of iron with cut threads, or of soft steel with our cold pressed and raised threads, and we recommend the latter as superior.

Weight of Plow Bolts.

Average Number in 100 lbs.

Length	$\frac{5}{16}$ inch	$\frac{3}{8}$ inch	$\frac{7}{16}$ inch	$\frac{1}{2}$ inch
1 inch	2,200	1,550	1,120	800
1¼ "	2,000	1,370	990	725
1½ "	1,820	1,250	890	665
1¾ "	1,680	1,160	810	610
2 "	1,580	1,080	750	565
2½ "	....	925	660	490
3 "	....	....	575	430

Tire Bolts.

Price per Hundred.

Length	$\frac{3}{16}$	$\frac{1}{4}$	$\frac{5}{16}$	$\frac{3}{8}$
1	.60	.80	1.10	2.20
1 $\frac{1}{4}$	.60	.80	1.10	2.20
1 $\frac{1}{2}$	.60	.80	1.10	2.20
1 $\frac{3}{4}$	.65	.85	1.10	2.20
2	.70	.90	1.17	2.20
2 $\frac{1}{4}$	.75	.95	1.24	2.30
2 $\frac{1}{2}$	.80	1.00	1.31	2.40
2 $\frac{3}{4}$	.85	1.05	1.38	2.50
3	.90	1.10	1.45	2.60
3 $\frac{1}{4}$	.95	1.15	1.52	2.70
3 $\frac{1}{2}$	1.00	1.20	1.59	2.80
3 $\frac{3}{4}$	1.05	1.25	1.66	2.90
4	1.10	1.30	1.73	3.00
4 $\frac{1}{4}$	1.15	1.35	1.80	3.10
4 $\frac{1}{2}$	1.20	1.40	1.87	3.20
4 $\frac{3}{4}$	1.25	1.45	1.94	3.30
5	1.30	1.50	2.01	3.40
5 $\frac{1}{2}$	1.40	1.60	2.15	3.60
6	1.50	1.70	2.29	3.80

The length of these Bolts is measured over all.

Fig. 14.

Belt or Elevator Bolts.

Price per Hundred.

Diameter	$\frac{3}{16}$ inch	$\frac{1}{4}$ inch	$\frac{5}{16}$ inch	$\frac{3}{8}$ inch
$\frac{3}{4}$ in. long	3.00	3.00	3.60	. .
1 "	3.10	3.10	3.70	4.40
1 $\frac{1}{4}$ "	3.20	3.20	3.80	4.55
1 $\frac{1}{2}$ "	3.30	3.30	3.90	4.70
1 $\frac{3}{4}$ "			4.00	4.85
2 "			. .	5.00

The length of these Bolts is measured over all.

Stud Bolts,

Either Iron or Steel.

With U. S. Standard Chamfered and Trimmed Hexagon Nuts.

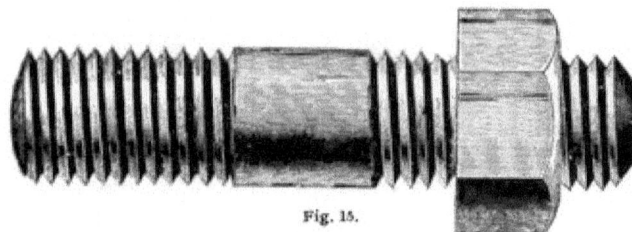

Fig. 15.

Price per Hundred.

Diam.	⅜	⁷⁄₁₆	½	⁹⁄₁₆	⅝	¾	⅞	1	1⅛	1¼
No. of Threads	16	14	13	12	11	10	9	8	7	7
1½ in.	4.00	5.10	5.50	..	..			..	..	..
1¾ ''	4.10	5.25	5.65	..	..	..	..	..	..	..
2 ''	4.20	5.40	5.80	8.50	8.50	12.40	..	..	..	..
2¼ ''	4.30	5.55	5.95	8.75	8.75	12.70	..	..	..	..
2½ ''	4.40	5.70	6.10	9.00	9.00	13.00	18.00	..	..	..
2¾ ''	4.50	5.85	6.25	9.25	9.25	13.30	18.50	..	..	..
3 ''	4.60	6.00	6.40	9.50	9.50	13.60	19.00	27.80	..	..
3¼ ''	4.70	6.15	6.55	9.75	9.75	13.90	19.50	28.40	..	..
3½ ''	4.80	6.30	6.70	10.00	10.00	14.20	20.00	29.00	..	..
3¾ ''	4.90	6.45	6.85	10.25	10.25	14.50	20.50	29.60	..	..
4 ''	5.00	6.60	7.00	10.50	10.50	14.80	21.00	30.20	43.00	60.00
4½ ''	5.25	6.90	7.30	11.00	11.00	15.40	22.00	31.40	44.50	62.50
5 ''	..	..	..	11.50	11.50	16.00	23.00	32.60	46.00	65.00
5½ ''	..	..	..	12.00	12.00	16.60	24.00	33.80	47.50	67.50
6 ''	..	..	..	12.50	12.50	17.20	25.00	35.00	49.00	70.00

The length of Stud Bolts is measured over all.
In ordering please give length of thread wanted on each end, and length of body, and state whether the blank part is wanted milled or rough.
The end having a short thread (tap end) has a tight fit and the other (nut end) a regular fit.
When Studs with Case-hardened or Semi-finished Nuts are ordered, the Nuts will be charged separately. (List prices on page 38).
These Studs can be furnished either of iron with cut threads, or of soft steel with our cold pressed and raised threads, and we recommend the latter as superior. Brass Studs at a special price.

Manufacturers' Standard List of

Forged Set Screws and Tap Bolts.

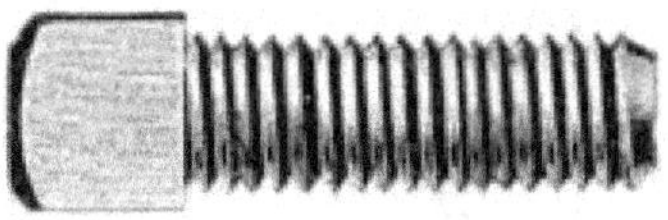

Fig. 16.

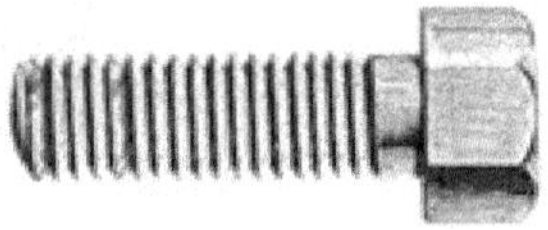

Fig 17.

Square Heads.—Price per Hundred.

Adopted January 30, 1895, to take effect February 14, 1895.

Dia. Screw	1/4	5/16	3/8	7/16	1/2	9/16 & 5/8	3/4	7/8	1
1 1/2	1.00	1.15	1.35	1.60	2.00	3.00	4.20	6.00	8.00
1 3/4	1.05	1.21	1.42	1.69	2.10	3.12	4.35	6.20	8.25
2	1.10	1.27	1.49	1.78	2.20	3.24	4.50	6.40	8.50
2 1/4	1.15	1.33	1.56	1.87	2.30	3.36	4.65	6.60	8.75
2 1/2	1.20	1.39	1.63	1.96	2.40	3.48	4.80	6.80	9.00
2 3/4	1.25	1.45	1.70	2.05	2.50	3.60	4.95	7.00	9.25
3	1.30	1.51	1.77	2.14	2.60	3.72	5.10	7.20	9.50
3 1/4	. .	1.57	1.84	2.23	2.70	3.84	5.25	7.40	9.75
3 1/2	. .	. .	1.91	2.32	2.80	3.96	5.40	7.60	10.00
3 3/4	. .	. .	. .	2.41	2.90	4.08	5.55	7.80	10.25
4	. .	. .	. .	. .	3 00	4.20	5.70	8.00	10.50

The following extra is to be understood as a part of this list:
With Hexagon Heads, 10 per cent. extra.
Heads of Tap Bolts are same sizes as heads of Machine Bolts. For these dimensions, as well as sizes of heads on Set Screws, see page 56.
In ordering 1/4-inch Screws state whether 12 or 13 threads per inch are wanted. If no instructions to the contrary are given, we will furnish U. S. Standard Threads.
The length of Set Screws and Tap Bolts is measured from under head to point.

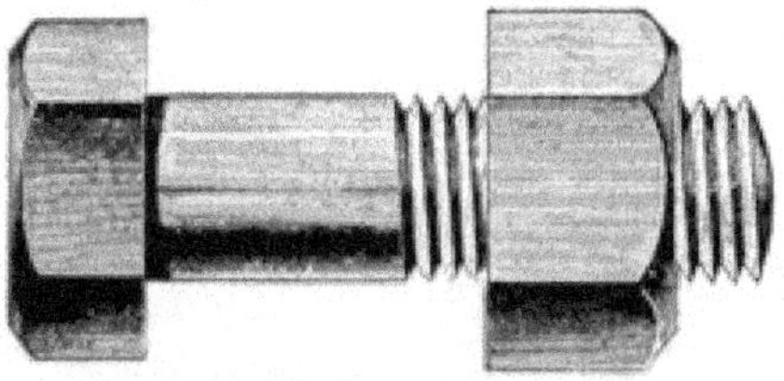

Fig. 18.

Milled Coupling Bolts.

Hexagon Heads and Hexagon Nuts.
Price per Hundred.

Diam. Screw	5/8	3/4	7/8	1	1 1/8	1 1/4
2	25.00	. .	. .	. .	. .	. .
2 1/2	26.50	32.00	38.75	. .	. .	. .
3	28.00	34.00	40.75	56.00	70.00	. .
3 1/2	29.50	36.00	42.75	58.00	73.00	100.00
4	31.00	38.00	44.75	60.00	76.00	105.00
4 1/2	. .	40.00	46.75	62.00	79.00	110.00
5	. .	. .	48.75	64.00	82.00	115.00
5 1/2	. .	. .	. .	66.00	85.00	120.00
6	. .	. .	. .	. .	88.00	125.00

These Bolts are made from best iron, with bodies turned and threaded, Heads and Nuts faced inside. Length is measured under head to point.
If wanted with Finished and Case-hardened Nuts, add difference in cost between Finished and Case-hardened, and Semi-finished Nuts, page 38.

Case Hardened Iron Set Screws.

Fig. 19.
Oval Point.

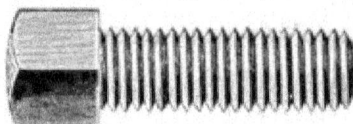

Fig. 20.

Fig. 21.
Cup Point.

Square Heads. Price per Hundred.

Diam. of Screw	¼	5/16	⅜	7/16	½	9/16	⅝	¾	⅞	1	1⅛	1¼
Threads to inch	20	18	16	14	13	12	11	10	9	8	7	7
¾	2.00	2.20	2.50	2.90	3.40	4.25	5.00					
1	2.15	2.35	2.65	3.10	3.60	4.25	5.00	7.00				
1¼	2.30	2.50	2.80	3.30	3.80	4.50	5.25	7.00	11.30			
1½	2.45	2.65	2.95	3.50	4.00	4.75	5.50	7.50	11.30	14.90		
1¾	2.60	2.80	3.10	3.70	4.20	5.00	5.75	8.00	12.00	15.90	19.50	
2	2.80	3.00	3.30	3.95	4.45	5.30	6.05	8.60	12.90	17.00	21.10	25.30
2¼	..	3.25	3.55	4.25	4.75	5.65	6.40	9.30	13.80	18.40	22.90	27.40
2½	..	..	3.85	4.60	5.10	6.05	6.80	10.00	14.80	19.80	24.70	29.60
2¾	..	..	..	5.00	5.50	6.50	7.25	10.80	15.90	21.40	26.70	32.00
3	..	..	..	..	5.95	7.00	7.75	11.70	17.10	23.00	28.80	34.60
3¼	..	..	..	..	..	7.55	8.35	12.70	18.40	24.70	31.00	37.40
3½	..	..	..	..	..	..	8.95	13.70	19.70	26.40	33.20	40.20
3¾	..	..	..	..	..	..	..	14.70	21.00	28.10	35.40	48.00
4	..	..	..	..	..	..	..	..	22.30	29.80	37.60	45.80
Add for ea. ¼ in.	25	30	35	45	50	55	60	1.00	1.30	1.70	2.20	2.80

In ordering Set Screws please state whether cup or oval points are wanted. If no directions are given, the former will be sent.

In ordering ½-inch Screws, state whether 12 or 13 threads per inch are wanted. If no instructions to the contrary are given we will furnish U. S. Standard Threads.

Steel Set Screws.

Case Hardened. Price per Hundred.

Diam. of Screw	¼	5/16	⅜	7/16	½	9/16	⅝	¾	⅞	1
Threads to inch	20	18	16	14	13	12	11	10	9	8
¾	2.50	2.75	3.10	3.60	4.25	5.30	6.25			
1	2.65	2.90	3.30	3.90	4.50	5.30	6.25	8.75		
1¼	2.85	3.10	3.50	4.15	4.75	5.60	6.55	8.75	14.10	
1½	3.05	3.30	3.70	4.40	5.00	5.90	6.90	9.35	14.10	18.60
1¾	3.25	3.50	3.90	4.65	5.25	6.25	7.25	10.00	15.00	19.80
2	3.50	3.75	4.15	4.95	5.55	6.60	7.60	10.75	16.10	21.25
2¼	3.80	4.05	4.45	5.30	5.90	7.05	8.00	11.60	17.25	23.00
2½	4.10	4.45	4.80	5.75	6.35	7.55	8.50	12.50	18.50	24.70
2¾	4.45	4.80	5.25	6.20	6.85	8.10	9.05	13.50	19.85	26.65
3	4.75	5.20	5.70	6.75	7.45	8.75	9.70	14.60	21.35	28.75
3¼	..	5.55	6.10	7.30	8.05	9.45	10.45	15.85	23.00	30.85
3½	..	..	6.55	7.90	8.70	10.15	11.20	17.10	24.60	33.25
3¾	..	..	..	8.50	9.35	10.85	11.95	18.35	26.25	35.15
4	..	..	..	..	9.95	11.50	12.70	19.60	27.85	37.25
Add for each ¼ inch	35	40	50	60	70	80	90	1.30	1.75	2.30

Our Set Screws, iron or steel, are first-class and threaded true to gauge. The length of all Set Screws is measured under head.

Square Head Cap Screws.

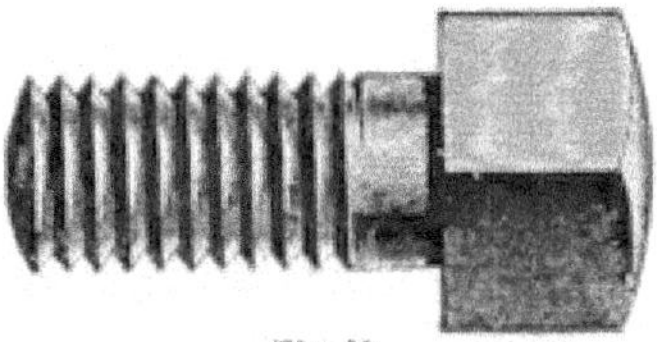

Fig 22.

Price per Hundred.

Diam. of Head	3/8	7/16	1/2	9/16	5/8	11/16	3/4	7/8	1 1/8	1 1/4	1 3/8	1 1/2	1 5/8
Length of Head	1/4	5/16	3/8	7/16	1/2	9/16	5/8	3/4	7/8	1	1 1/8	1 1/4	1 3/8
Diam. of Screw	1/4	5/16	3/8	7/16	1/2	9/16	5/8	3/4	7/8	1	1 1/8	1 1/4	1 3/8
3/4	2.40	2.75	3.20	3.80	4.40	5.75	. .	. .	. .	. .	. .	. .	. .
1	2.60	2.95	3.40	4.00	4.70	5.75	7.70	. .	. .	. .	. .	. .	. .
1 1/4	2.75	3.10	3.65	4.20	4.95	6.05	7.70	10.50	. .	. .	. .	. .	. .
1 1/2	2.90	3.30	3.85	4.45	5.25	6.35	8.25	10.50	14.00	. .	. .	. .	. .
1 3/4	3.05	3.50	4.10	4.70	5.55	6.65	8.80	11.10	14.80	18.00	. .	. .	. .
2	3.25	3.70	4.35	4.95	5.90	7.05	9.40	11.80	15.70	19.00	22.50	. .	. .
2 1/4	. .	4.00	4.65	5.25	6.30	7.55	10.10	12.60	16.70	20.20	24.00	30.00	. .
2 1/2	. .	. .	5.00	5.60	6.75	8.15	10.90	13.50	17.80	21.50	25.80	32.00	39.00
2 3/4	. .	. .	. .	6.00	7.25	8.85	11.80	14.60	19.10	23.10	27.90	34.20	41.50
3	. .	. .	. .	. .	7.80	9.65	12.80	15.90	20.60	25.00	30.50	37.00	45.00
Threads to inch	20	18	16	14	13	12	11	10	9	8	7	7	6
Add for ea. 1/4 in.	25	35	45	55	65	90	1.20	1.50	1.80	2.30	3.00	3.50	4.00

Hexagon Head Cap Screws.

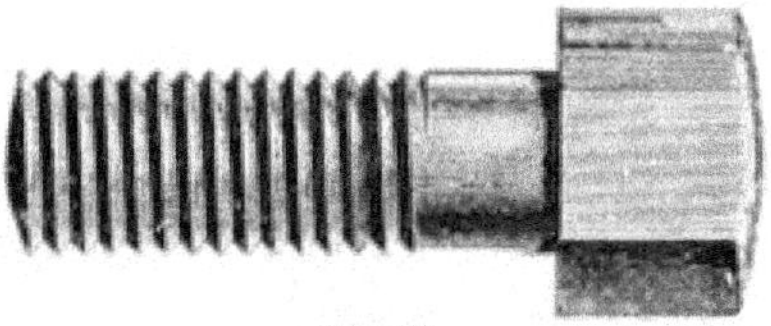

Fig. 23.

Price per Hundred.

Diam. of Head	3/8	1/2	9/16	5/8	3/4	13/16	7/8	1	1 1/8	1 1/4	1 3/8	1 1/2
Length of Head	1/4	5/16	3/8	7/16	1/2	9/16	5/8	3/4	7/8	1	1 1/8	1 1/4
Diam. of Screw	1/4	5/16	3/8	7/16	1/2	9/16	5/8	3/4	7/8	1	1 1/8	1 1/4
3/4	3.00	3.25	3.75	4.40	5.50	7.00	. .	. .	. .	. .	. .	. .
1	3.25	3.50	4.00	4.70	5.70	7.00	9.50	. .	. .	. .	. .	. .
1 1/4	3.50	3.75	4.25	5.00	6.00	7.50	9.50	12.20	. .	. .	. .	. .
1 1/2	3.75	4.00	4.50	5.30	6.30	8.00	10.00	12.20	16.00	. .	. .	. .
1 3/4	4.00	4.25	4.75	5.60	6.60	8.50	10.60	12.80	16.60	21.20	. .	. .
2	4.25	4.60	5.05	5.95	7.00	9.10	11.20	13.40	17.20	22.30	29.00	37.50
2 1/4	. .	5.00	5.40	6.35	7.50	9.70	11.90	14.10	17.90	23.60	30.50	39.30
2 1/2	. .	. .	5.80	6.80	8.00	10.40	12.70	14.90	18.80	25.10	32.30	41.40
2 3/4	. .	. .	. .	7.30	8.60	11.20	13.60	15.90	20.00	26.90	34.40	44.00
3	. .	. .	. .	. .	9.30	12.10	14.70	17.00	21.80	29.00	37.00	47.50
Threads to inch	20	18	16	14	13	12	11	10	9	8	7	7
Add for ea. 1/4 in.	30	40	50	60	80	1.00	1.30	1.60	2.00	2.40	3.00	4.00

In ordering Screws 1/2 inch diameter always state whether wanted with 12 or 13 threads.
All Screws sent with United States Standard Threads unless otherwise ordered.
The length of all Cap Screws is measured under head.

Railroad Track Bolts.

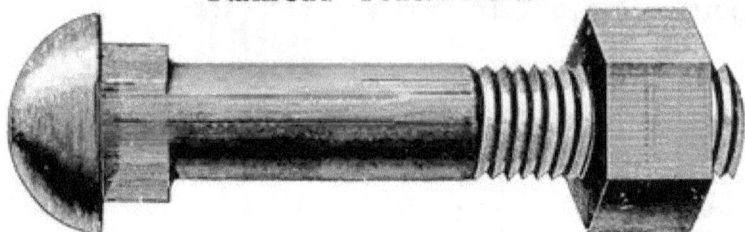

Fig. 24.

We make Iron Cut Thread Track Bolts of superior quality,
giving special attention to uniformity of threads and fit of nuts. In this department of our works we have extensive facilities and are able to make prompt
shipments.

We are prepared also to make and ship promptly,

COILED STEEL SPRING NUT LOCKS,

Fig. 25.

hardened and tempered in oil, prices for which we shall be glad to quote on
receipt of inquiry.

We are also the exclusive manufacturers in the East, of the celebrated

HARVEY PATENT GRIP THREAD TRACK BOLT,

pronounced by many railroad men the best track bolt they have ever used,
especially when fitted with our Ideal Nut.

Fig. 26.

Please note the principal features of this Bolt and Nut.

1st. The Bolt has a ratchet thread undercut on the bearing side, or about five
degrees *less* than a right angle to the axis of the bolt, and the apex of the thread
is cut to a knife edge.

2d. The Nut also has a ratchet thread, the bearing side of which is about
five degrees *greater* than a right angle to the axis of the nut. Thus there is a

cavity of about ten degrees between the bolt thread and the nut thread ; and when the nut is screwed up tight against the angle bar, the strain forces the thin bolt threads out into the nut threads, completely filling the cavity referred to, which makes a perfect fit and locks the nut so that *it will never work loose.*

3rd.   The Ideal Nut has the corners off, as shown in the cut (page 27), for use on angle bars as a substitute for hexagon nuts, and is made about $\frac{1}{16}$ thicker than the diameter of the bolt, and has a recess $\frac{3}{16}$ deep cut in its bearing face, which recess is a little greater in diameter than the bolt and is intended to enclose and protect the bolt threads from injury by the rubbing or pounding action of the angle plate in service, thus insuring two good threads to tighten the nut on when the joint becomes loose from wear or stretch of the bolt.

4th.   Thus the Bolt and Nut form a complete fastening in themselves—only two pieces—as simple as possible ; (no nut locks, springs, keys, washers, wires, or other complications): are cheaper and better than ordinary bolts fitted with spring washers, and being made of *best Iron* are warranted in all respects first-class and entirely satisfactory.

Notwithstanding the superior merits of our iron cut thread Harvey Grip Bolts, we now produce a soft steel Track Bolt without cutting the threads at all, by a new process of raising the threads above the body of the bolt by cold pressure, illustrated herewith.

These bolts have more than fifty per cent. greater tensile strength than iron cut thread bolts of same size, and are actually stronger in the threaded portion than in the shank, as shown by hundreds of tensile tests made by us.

No metal is cut out by our process of threading these bolts, but the thread is raised or spun up above the surface of the shank, so that the diameter of the threaded portion is about $\frac{1}{16}$ inch greater than the shank, as shown in the cut.

Registered
"HARVEY GRIP"
Trade Mark

Registered "IDEAL" Trade Mark

Fig. 27.

HARVEY GRIP BOLT.   IDEAL NUT.

Made under Patents Dated

Made under Patents Dated

May 4, 1886.

Dec. 13, 1881.   Nov. 13, 1888.

Apr. 19, 1887.   Dec. 4, 1888.

Much of the best track in the United States is laid with these Bolts.

For the purpose of comparison with iron bolts having the ordinary cut threads we have had numerous tests made by Fairbanks & Co., of Philadelphia, and R. W. Hunt & Co., of Chicago, and we submit the following statement, which gives the average Tensile Strength, Elastic Limit, and Elongation of each kind of Bolt. We call your attention to the great excess of these three good qualities which are shown by our new process Cold Pressed Grip Thread Steel Bolts over common iron cut thread bolts of same size :

The average breaking strain of a $\frac{3}{4}''$ x $4''$ cold pressed grip thread steel bolt is . . . . 28,639 lbs.

The average breaking strain of a $\frac{3}{4}''$ x $4''$ good iron bolt with ordinary threads is . . . . 17,615 "

Showing in favor of the first 62 per cent., or . . . . 11,024 lbs.

The average elastic limit of a $\frac{3}{4}''$ x $4''$ cold pressed grip thread steel bolt is . . . . 20,201 lbs.

The average elastic limit of a $\frac{3}{4}''$ x $4''$ good iron bolt with ordinary threads is . . . . 12,750 "

Showing in favor of the first 58 per cent., or . . . . 7,451 lbs.

The average elongation before breaking of a $\frac{3}{4}''$ x $4''$ cold pressed grip thread steel bolt is . . . . 5-8 inch

The average elongation before breaking of a $\frac{3}{4}''$ x $4''$ good iron bolt with ordinary threads is . . . . 1-8 "

Showing in favor of the first . . . . 4-8 inch.

This comparison shows the tensile strength of our Soft Steel Cold Pressed Thread Bolts to be far greater than Iron Cut Thread Bolts of same diameter, partly because the latter have much of their strength cut away in threading.

These steel bolts broke in every instance in the shank of the bolt itself, as per cut below, leaving the threaded portion as perfect as when put under stress.

This cut shows great reduction in area at point of fracture, caused by elongation of the bolt under tensile strain.

Fig. 26.

We consider this showing very remarkable, indicating the great superiority of our Cold Pressed Thread Harvey Grip Steel Bolt in the three important qualities of **Tensile Strength, Elastic Limit,** and **Elongation.** In fact, we consider the soft steel bolt as much superior to the ordinary iron bolt with cut thread as steel rails are superior to iron rails.

Engineers in charge of maintenance of way will therefore please note that we are able to furnish these soft steel track bolts having at least 50 per cent. more strength than ¾ inch iron cut thread bolts ; and that these bolts will not begin to stretch except under a strain of about 20,000 pounds, while the iron bolts will begin to stretch at about 12,500 pounds ; and that the stretch of the steel bolt before breaking is about ⅝ inch, while the stretch of the iron bolt is only about ⅛ inch.

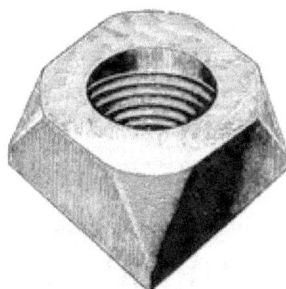

Fig. 29.

Our **Patent Ideal Nut** has the corners off for use on angle bars (preferable to hexagon nuts), and is made about $\frac{1}{16}$ inch thicker than other nuts, and has a recess in its bearing face a little greater in diameter than the bolt, intended to enclose or house the bolt threads and protect them from injury by the chafing of the plates in service.

In conclusion, our Soft Steel Harvey Grip Cold Pressed Thread Track Bolts with Ideal Nuts, covered by several patents, represent the highest point of perfection yet reached, and in comparison we regard the old-fashioned iron bolt, with much of its strength cut away in threading, as emphatically a "back number." We shall be pleased to forward samples for testing if desired.

The large capacity of our Rolling Mills enables us to supply promptly the wants of our Bolt, Nut and Rivet Departments ; hence we can execute all orders entrusted to us with promptness.

Steel Boiler Bolts.

With Cone Points, and fitted with our
Patent Recessed Square Nuts.

Price per Hundred.

Fig. 30.

Length under Head	½	⅝	¾	⅞
1 ½	6.00	9.00	12.70	18.80
2	6.35	9.55	13.45	19.80
2 ½	6.70	10.10	14.20	20.80
3	7.05	10.65	14.95	21.80
3 ½	7.40	11.20	15.70	22.80
4	7.75	11.75	16.45	23.80
4 ½	8.10	12.30	17.20	24.80
5	8.45	12.85	17.95	25.80

These bolts are made of soft steel with quite coarse threads, so that the nuts can be run on or off quickly by hand, and are fitted with our patent recessed nuts and will be found of great convenience to boiler-makers, being much better adapted for "fitting up bolts" than the ordinary machine bolts.

Boiler Stay Bolts.

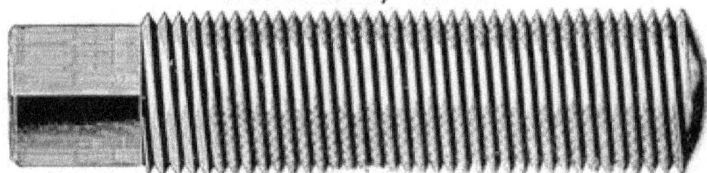

Fig. 31.

12 Threads per inch.—Price per Hundred.

Length under Head	⅞	1⅛ & ½	1⅛ & 1
2 ½	14.20	20.80	30.10
3	14.95	21.80	31.40
3 ½	15.70	22.80	32.70
4	16.45	23.80	34.00
4 ½	17.20	24.80	35.30
5	17.95	25.80	36.60
5 ½	18.70	26.80	37.90
6	19.45	27.80	39.20
6 ½	20.20	28.80	40.50
7	20.95	29.80	41.80
7 ½	21.70	30.80	43.10
8	22.50	31.80	44.40
9	24.00	33.80	47.00
10	25.50	35.80	49.60
11	27.00	37.80	52.20
12	28.50	39.80	54.80
Longer than 12 in., per lb.	.18	.16	.15

We are prepared to furnish a superior quality of double refined iron, rolled round and true to size, intended for Stay Bolts, and shall be glad to quote prices on application.
We invite the attention of Railway Master Mechanics to this material. It compares favorably with the best English or Norway stay bolt iron.

Boiler Patch Bolts.

(OR TAP RIVETS.)

Fig. 32.

Fig. 33.

Fig. 34.

Diameter	Length	PRICE EACH* for small lots		PRICE PER LB.** in lots of 25 lbs. or more	
		Blank	Cut	Blank	Cut
1/2 inch	1/2 to 1 inch	.04	.05	.25	.33
9/16 "	5/8 " 1 1/4 "	.05	.06	.22	.29
5/8 "	3/4 " 1 1/2 "	.05	.06	.20	.26
11/16 "	3/4 " 1 1/2 "	.06	.07	.20	.26
3/4 "	7/8 " 2 "	.07	.08	.19	.24
13/16 "	1 " 2 "	.09	.11	.19	.24
7/8 "	1 " 2 "	.10	.12	.18	.22
15/16 "	1 " 2 "	.13	.15	.18	.22
1 "	1 " 2 1/2 "	.15	.17	.17	.20
1 1/16 "	1 " 2 1/2 "	.18	.21	.17	.20
1 1/8 "	1 " 2 1/2 "	.18	.21	.17	.20
1 1/4 "	1 " 2 1/2 "	.22	.25	.17	.20

*Of greater length than specified, at special prices.
**Patch Bolts of shorter length are charged at 2 cents per lb. advance.

Please state, when threaded Patch Bolts are required, whether they are to be cut to U. S. Standard gauge, or 12 threads to the inch. Unless otherwise ordered, 12 threads cut on all Patch Bolts.

If cut with a special thread in small quantities, an extra charge will be made.

Heads countersunk at an angle of 45 degrees. To avoid misunderstanding order above bolts by referring to figure number.

Boiler Patch Bolts.

Average Number in 100 lbs.

Rivets.

Our Trade Mark, the letter "S," is stamped on
the head of each Rivet.

Fig. 35.   Fig. 37.   Fig. 36.

We are headquarters for everything in the line of
BOILER, BRIDGE, SHIP and TANK RIVETS,

our Reading Works, formerly operated by Messrs. J. H. Sternbergh &
Son, having given special attention to this branch of manufacture for
many years, turning out thousands of tons annually. While the bulk
of the rivets we make are 1-2″ and larger diameters, we manufacture
considerable quantities of Tank Rivets, 7-16, 3-8, 5-16, and 1-4″ diameters. All of our rivets are made in solid dies with heads central and
of such proportions as long experience has shown to be the most suitable.

We have from time to time tested various high grades of iron and
steel of foreign as well as American make, but have never found any-
thing better adapted to the manufacture of boiler and structural rivets
than the materials we use for that purpose ourselves, rolled to exact
sizes in our own works. We furnish either iron or steel Boiler Rivets,
as may be specified by our customers.

The uniformly excellent quality and finish of our Boiler Rivets,
widely known as Sternbergh Boiler Rivets, has earned for them an envi-
able reputation—our customers pronounce them absolutely the best
made in the country—and we have no hesitation in guaranteeing them
to give entire satisfaction.

We shall be glad to send a small quantity free of charge to any
boilermaker unacquainted with their quality, who may wish to test
them in comparison with any other make in the market. We know
that our rivets will speak for themselves.

Probably nine-tenths of all the rivets used in the building of our
new war vessels were made by our Reading Works. We have supplied
large quantities of these rivets not only to the United States Government direct, but to private ship yards building Government
vessels, and are prepared to meet all reasonable specifications.

Boiler Rivets.

Shearing and Tensile Strength in Pounds.

	1/2 in.	5/8 in.	11/16 in.	3/4 in.	7/8 in.
Shearing	9.225	13.150	18.000	20.525	27.100
Tensile	10.600	16.500	20.000	23.800	31.400

The elongation of our Boiler Rivet Rods is from 30 to 34 per cent. in eight inches. Tensile strength per square inch about 50,000 pounds.

In ordering Rivets please specify the diameter first, then the length, thus: 3/4×1 1/2 inches, so that we may not misunderstand what is wanted.

Unless otherwise expressed we shall understand that a keg of Rivets means 100 pounds.

The length of Countersunk Rivets is understood to be "out to out," all others from under the head.

Table

Showing the Average Number of Cone Head Rivets of Enumerated Sizes in 100 Pounds, when made in Solid Dies.

Length	3/8	7/16	1/2	5/8	11/16	3/4	7/8	Length	3/8	7/16	1/2	5/8	11/16	3/4	7/8
3/4	2373	1476	1103	642	..	..	..	3 1/2	837	548	433	270	208	177	126
7/8	2190	1371	1030	604	..	..	..	3/4	791	519	411	257	198	168	120
1	2034	1280	968	571	400	345	..	4	749	490	390	244	189	161	115
1/8	1898	1200	910	541	382	322	..	1/4	..	..	372	233	180	155	110
1/4	1780	1129	862	514	365	311	..	1/2	..	..	355	223	172	149	105
3/8	1675	1066	815	489	350	295	..	3/4	..	..	339	214	166	143	101
1/2	1582	1010	776	462	335	284	207	5	..	..	325	205	160	136	97
5/8	1498	960	740	446	324	275	199	1/4	..	..	312	197	154	131	94
3/4	1424	914	707	428	311	266	192	1/2	..	..	300	190	149	127	91
7/8	1356	872	672	411	302	257	185	3/4	..	..	289	183	144	123	88
2	1295	834	648	395	293	249	178	6	..	..	279	177	139	118	85
1/8	1238	800	623	381	285	240	172	1/4	..	..	..	171	135	114	82
1/4	1187	768	599	367	277	233	167	1/2	..	..	..	165	131	110	79
3/8	1139	738	577	354	269	226	162	3/4	..	..	..	160	127	107	77
1/2	1095	711	556	343	261	219	157	7	..	..	..	155	123	104	75
5/8	1052	687	537	332	253	212	152	1/4	..	..	..	150	119	100	73
3/4	1017	662	519	321	245	206	148	1/2	..	..	..	146	116	97	71
7/8	982	636	503	311	237	201	144	3/4	..	..	..	142	113	94	69
3	949	611	487	302	230	196	140	8	..	..	..	138	110	92	67
1/4	890	581	459	285	218	186	132	..	..	..	..	..	..	..	..

U. S. STANDARD

Chamfered, Trimmed and Reamed Nuts.

Fig. 38.

Fig. 39.

Short Diam.	Thickness	Hole	Size Bolt	SQUARE			HEXAGON		
				Price per lb. Blank	Price per lb. Tapped	Av. No. in 100 lbs. Blank	Price per lb. Blank	Price per lb. Tapped	Av. No. in 100 lbs. Blank
$\frac{1}{2}$	$\frac{1}{4}$	.185= $\frac{3}{16}$ scant	$\frac{1}{4}$	20.0	22.0	7400	27.0	29.5	8880
$\frac{11}{16}$	$\frac{5}{16}$	.240= $\frac{1}{4}$ scant	$\frac{5}{16}$	18.0	19.5	4000	24.0	26.0	4800
$\frac{13}{16}$	$\frac{3}{8}$	.294= $\frac{19}{64}$ scant	$\frac{3}{8}$	14.5	15.6	2730	18.5	20.1	3276
$\frac{15}{16}$	$\frac{7}{16}$	.344= $\frac{11}{32}$	$\frac{7}{16}$	14.0	14.9	1700	18.0	19.3	2040
$\frac{7}{8}$	$\frac{1}{2}$	.400= $\frac{13}{32}$ scant	$\frac{1}{2}$	11.3	12.0	1160	14.0	15.0	1392
$\frac{31}{32}$	$\frac{9}{16}$	.454= $\frac{29}{64}$	$\frac{9}{16}$	11.3	11.9	900	14.0	14.9	1080
$1\frac{1}{16}$	$\frac{5}{8}$	.507= $\frac{1}{2}$ full	$\frac{5}{8}$	10.0	10.5	653	12.5	13.2	784
$1\frac{1}{4}$	$\frac{3}{4}$	.620= $\frac{5}{8}$ scant	$\frac{3}{4}$	9.4	9.8	386	10.9	11.5	463
$1\frac{7}{16}$	$\frac{7}{8}$	.731= $\frac{11}{16}$ scant	$\frac{7}{8}$	9.4	9.8	260	10.9	11.5	312
$1\frac{5}{8}$	1	.837= $\frac{27}{32}$ scant	1	9.4	9.8	170	10.9	11.5	204
$1\frac{13}{16}$	$1\frac{1}{8}$	.940= $\frac{15}{16}$ full	$1\frac{1}{8}$	9.4	9.8	122	10.9	11.5	146
2	$1\frac{1}{4}$	1.065= $1\frac{1}{16}$ full	$1\frac{1}{4}$	10.1	10.5	90	11.5	12.1	108
$2\frac{3}{16}$	$1\frac{3}{8}$	1.160= $1\frac{5}{32}$ full	$1\frac{3}{8}$	10.3	10.8	69	12.0	12.7	83
$2\frac{3}{8}$	$1\frac{1}{2}$	1.284= $1\frac{9}{32}$ full	$1\frac{1}{2}$	10.7	11.3	54	12.6	13.4	65
$2\frac{9}{16}$	$1\frac{5}{8}$	1.389= $1\frac{25}{64}$ scant	$1\frac{5}{8}$	11.1	11.8	43	13.2	14.1	52
$2\frac{3}{4}$	$1\frac{3}{4}$	1.491= $1\frac{1}{2}$ scant	$1\frac{3}{4}$	11.5	12.2	35	14.0	14.9	42
$2\frac{15}{16}$	$1\frac{7}{8}$	1.616= $1\frac{5}{8}$ scant	$1\frac{7}{8}$	12.0	12.8	29	14.5	15.5	35
$3\frac{1}{8}$	2	1.712= $1\frac{23}{32}$ scant	2	12.0	12.9	24	14.5	15.6	29
$3\frac{5}{16}$	$2\frac{1}{8}$	1.836= $1\frac{27}{32}$ scant	$2\frac{1}{8}$	12.5	13.5	$20\frac{1}{2}$	15.0	16.2	26
$3\frac{1}{2}$	$2\frac{1}{4}$	1.962= $1\frac{31}{32}$ full	$2\frac{1}{4}$	12.5	13.6	17	15.0	16.3	23
$3\frac{11}{16}$	$2\frac{3}{8}$	2.080= $2\frac{5}{64}$ full	$2\frac{3}{8}$	13.5	14.7	15	16.0	17.4	20
$3\frac{7}{8}$	$2\frac{1}{2}$	2.176= $2\frac{11}{64}$ full	$2\frac{1}{2}$	13.5	14.8	12	16.0	17.5	16

These are *extra fine* unfinished nuts, cupped and trimmed outside to exact dimensions, and have *reamed holes*, at right angles to their bases, to suit U. S. Standard Taps, and are in all respects a superior article.

We make both Hot-punched and Cold-punched Chamfered, Trimmed and Reamed Nuts ; and the above list applies to both kinds.

For less than keg lots (200 pounds) of a size, the following extras will be charged, viz :

At the rate of 20 cents per 100 pounds for 100 pounds or more.

At the rate of 50 cents per 100 pounds for less than 100 pounds.

In ordering Cold-punched Nuts always state whether Plain or Chamfered, Trimmed and Reamed Nuts are required.

U. S. STANDARD

Plain Cold-Punched Nuts.

Fig. 40.

Fig. 41.

Width	Thickness	Hole	Bolt	Square: Price per lb. Blank	Square: Price per lb. Tapped	Square: Av. No. in 100 lbs. Blank	Hexagon: Price per lb. Blank	Hexagon: Price per lb. Tapped	Hexagon: Av. No. in 100 lbs. Blank
1/2	1/4	.185= 3/16 scant	1/4	13.8	15.8	6700	21.0	23.5	7500
19/32	5/16	.240= 1/4 scant	5/16	12.8	14.3	4100	19.0	21.0	4700
11/16	3/8	.294= 19/64 scant	3/8	11.0	12.1	2400	14.7	16.3	2800
25/32	7/16	.344= 11/32	7/16	10.5	11.4	1550	13.7	15.0	1830
7/8	1/2	.400= 13/32 scant	1/2	9.3	10.0	1100	11.5	12.5	1300
31/32	9/16	.454= 29/64	9/16	9.3	9.9	825	11.5	12.4	990
1 1/16	5/8	.507= 1/2 full	5/8	8.9	9.4	580	10.7	11.4	700
1 1/4	3/4	.620= 5/8 scant	3/4	8.6	9.0	348	10.2	10.8	438
1 7/16	7/8	.731= 47/64 scant	7/8	8.6	9.0	228	10.2	10.8	290
1 5/8	1	.837= 27/32 scant	1	8.4	8.8	156	10.0	10.6	198
1 13/16	1 1/8	.940= 15/16 full	1 1/8	8.4	8.8	122	10.0	10.6	140
2	1 1/4	1.065=1 1/16 full	1 1/4	8.8	9.2	88	10.5	11.1	103
2 3/16	1 3/8	1.160=1 5/32 full	1 3/8	8.8	9.3	65	10.5	11.2	77
2 3/8	1 1/2	1.284=1 9/32 full	1 1/2	9.6	10.2	54	11.3	12.1	63
2 9/16	1 5/8	1.389=1 25/64 scant	1 5/8	9.6	10.3	42	11.3	12.2	50
2 3/4	1 3/4	1.491=1 1/2 scant	1 3/4	10.2	10.9	33	12.1	13.0	39
2 15/16	1 7/8	1.616=1 5/8 scant	1 7/8	10.2	11.0	27	12.1	13.1	31
3 1/8	2	1.712=1 23/32 scant	2	10.6	11.5	23	12.6	13.7	28
3 5/16	2 1/8	1.836=1 27/32 scant	2 1/8	11.0	12.0	19	13.0	14.2	24
3 1/2	2 1/4	1.962=1 31/32 scant	2 1/4	11.5	12.6	17	13.5	14.8	20

For less than keg lots (200 pounds) of a size, the following extras will be charged, viz:

At the rate of 20 cents per 100 pounds for 100 pounds or more.

At the rate of 50 cents per 100 pounds for less than 100 pounds.

In ordering Cold-Punched Nuts always state whether Plain or Chamfered, Trimmed and Reamed Nuts are required.

U. S. STANDARD

Hot-Pressed Square and Hexagon Nuts

and

Hot-Pressed Reamed Square and Hexagon Nuts.

Fig. 42.

Fig. 43.

Short Dia.	Thickness	Hole	Size Bolt	Square — Price per Pound — Hot-Pressed Blank	Square — Hot-Pressed Tapped	Square — Ream'd Blank	Hexagon — Price per Pound — Hot-Pressed Blank	Hexagon — Hot-Pressed Tapped	Hexagon — Ream'd Blank
1/2	1/4	.185= 3/16 scant	1/4	13.0	15.0	13.8	20.0	22.5	21.0
19/32	5/16	.240= 1/4 scant	5/16	12.0	13.5	12.8	18.0	20.0	19.0
11/16	3/8	.294= 19/64 scant	3/8	10.5	11.6	11.0	14.0	15.6	14.7
25/32	7/16	.344= 11/32	7/16	10.0	10.9	10.5	13.0	14.3	13.7
7/8	1/2	.400= 13/32 scant	1/2	9.0	9.7	9.3	11.2	12.2	11.6
31/32	9/16	.454= 29/64	9/16	9.0	9.6	9.3	11.2	12.1	11.5
1 1/16	5/8	.507= 1/2 full	5/8	8.7	9.2	8.9	10.5	11.2	10.7
1 1/4	3/4	.620= 5/8 scant	3/4	8.5	8.9	8.6	10.0	10.6	10.2
1 7/16	7/8	.731= 47/64 scant	7/8	8.4	8.8	8.6	9.9	10.5	10.2
1 5/8	1	.837= 27/32 scant	1	8.2	8.6	8.4	9.7	10.3	10.0
1 13/16	1 1/8	.940= 15/16 full	1 1/8	8.2	8.6	8.4	9.7	10.3	10.0
2	1 1/4	1.065=1 1/16 full	1 1/4	8.4	8.8	8.8	9.9	10.5	10.5
2 3/16	1 3/8	1.160=1 5/32 full	1 3/8	8.5	9.0	8.8	10.0	10.7	10.5
2 3/8	1 1/2	1.284=1 9/32 full	1 1/2	8.8	9.4	9.6	10.3	11.1	11.3
2 9/16	1 5/8	1.389=1 25/64 scant	1 5/8	9.0	9.7	9.6	10.5	11.4	11.3
2 3/4	1 3/4	1.491=1 1/2 scant	1 3/4	9.3	10.0	10.2	10.8	11.7	12.1
2 15/16	1 7/8	1.616=1 5/8 scant	1 7/8	9.5	10.3	10.2	11.0	12.0	12.1
3 1/8	2	1.712=1 23/32 scant	2	9.7	10.6	10.6	11.2	12.3	12.6
3 5/16	2 1/8	1.836=1 27/32 scant	2 1/8	10.0	11.0	11.0	11.7	12.9	13.0
3 1/2	2 1/4	1.962=1 31/32 scant	2 1/4	10.0	11.1	11.5	11.7	13.0	13.5
3 11/16	2 3/8	2.086=2 3/32 scant	2 3/8	10.3	11.5	12.0	12.2	13.6	14.0
3 7/8	2 1/2	2 3/16	2 1/2	10.5	11.8	12.2	12.4	13.9	14.2
4 1/4	2 3/4	2 7/16	2 3/4	11.0	12.4	12.7	13.0	14.6	15.0
4 5/8	3	2 11/16	3	11.5	13.0	13.2	13.5	15.2	15.6

For less than keg lots (200 pounds) of a size the following extras will be charged, viz.:

At the rate of 20 cents per 100 pounds for 100 pounds or more.

At the rate of 50 cents per 100 pounds for less than 100 pounds.

Manufacturers' Standard

Square and Hexagon Hot-Pressed Nuts.

Fig. 44.

Fig. 45.

Square						Hexagon					
Short Dia.	Thickness	Hole	Size Bolt	Price per lb. Blank	Price per lb. Tapped	Short Dia.	Thickness	Hole	Size Bolt	Price per lb. Blank	Price per lb. Tapped
1/2	1/4	7/32	1/4	13.0	15.0	1/2	1/4	7/32	1/4	20.0	22.5
5/8	5/16	9/32	5/16	11.5	13.0	5/8	5/16	9/32	5/16	16.0	18.0
3/4	3/8	11/32	3/8	10.0	11.1	3/4	3/8	11/32	3/8	13.0	14.6
7/8	7/16	23/64	7/16	9.2	10.1	7/8	7/16	23/64	7/16	11.4	12.7
1	1/2	7/16	1/2	8.7	9.4	1	1/2	7/16	1/2	10.5	11.5
1 1/8	9/16	1/2	9/16	8.6	9.2	1 1/8	9/16	1/2	9/16	10.4	11.3
1 1/4	5/8	9/16	5/8	8.5	9.0	1 1/4	5/8	9/16	5/8	10.1	10.8
1 1/2	3/4	21/32	3/4	8.4	8.8	1 3/8	3/4	21/32	3/4	9.9	10.5
1 3/4	7/8	25/32	7/8	8.3	8.7	1 5/8	7/8	25/32	7/8	9.8	10.4
2	1	7/8	1	8.2	8.6	1 3/4	1	7/8	1	9.7	10.3
2 1/4	1 1/8	31/32	1 1/8	8.2	8.6	2	1 1/8	31/32	1 1/8	9.7	10.3
2 3/8	1 1/4	1 3/32	1 1/4	8.3	8.7	2 1/8	1 1/4	1 3/32	1 1/4	9.8	10.4
2 3/4	1 3/8	1 3/16	1 3/8	8.5	9.0	2 1/2	1 3/8	1 3/16	1 3/8	10.0	10.7
3	1 1/2	1 5/16	1 1/2	8.7	9.3	2 3/4	1 1/2	1 5/16	1 1/2	10.2	11.0
3 1/4	1 5/8	1 7/16	1 5/8	8.9	9.6	3	1 5/8	1 7/16	1 5/8	10.4	11.3
3 1/2	1 3/4	1 9/16	1 3/4	9.2	9.9	3 1/4	1 3/4	1 9/16	1 3/4	10.7	11.6
3 3/4	1 7/8	1 11/16	1 7/8	9.4	10.2	3 1/2	2	1 11/16	1 7/8	10.9	11.9
4	2	1 13/16	2	9.6	10.5	3 1/2	2	1 13/16	2	11.1	12.2
4	2 1/8	1 7/8	2 1/8	9.7	10.7	3 3/4	2 1/8	1 7/8	2 1/8	11.4	12.6
4 1/4	2 1/4	2	2 1/4	9.9	11.0	3 3/4	2 1/4	2	2 1/4	11.6	12.9
4 1/2	2 3/8	2 1/8	2 3/8	10.1	11.3	4	2 3/8	2 1/8	2 3/8	12.0	13.4
4 1/2	2 1/2	2 1/4	2 1/2	. .	. .	4 1/4	2 1/2	2 1/4	2 1/2	. .	. .
4 3/4	2 3/4	2 7/16	2 3/4	. .	. .	4 1/2	2 3/4	2 7/16	2 3/4	. .	. .
5	3	2 11/16	3	. .	. .	4 3/4	3	2 11/16	3	. .	. .
5 1/2	3 1/4	2 15/16	3 1/4	. .	.	5	3 1/4	2 15/16	3 1/4	. .	. .
6	3 1/2	3 1/8	3 1/2	. .	. .	5 1/4	3 1/2	3 1/8	3 1/2	. .	. .

For less than keg lots (200 pounds) of a size the following extras will be charged, viz.:

At the rate of 20 cents per 100 pounds for 100 pounds or more.

At the rate of 50 cents per 100 pounds for less than 100 pounds.

In ordering nuts other than U. S. Standard sizes, always give short diameter, thickness, and size of hole wanted.

Manufacturers' Standard

Square and Hexagon Hot-Pressed Nuts.

Fig. 46.

Fig. 47.

NARROW-GAUGE SIZES.

SQUARE						HEXAGON					
Short Dia.	Thickness	Hole	Size Bolt	Price per lb. Blank	Price per lb. Tapp'd	Short Dia.	Thickness	Hole	Size Bolt	Price per lb. Blank	Price per lb. Tapp'd
13/32	3/16	7/32	1/8	20.0	24.5						
15/32	7/32	1/4	1/4	13.7	15.7						
1/16	9/32	5/16	5/16	12.3	13.8						
11/16	5/16	21/64	3/8	10.7	11.8	11/16	3/8	21/64	3/8	14.0	15.6
13/16	7/16	27/64	7/16	10.0	10.9	13/16	7/16	27/64	7/16	13.0	14.3
7/8	7/16	15/32	1/2	9.0	9.7	7/8	1/2	15/32	1/2	11.2	12.2
1	9/16	9/16	9/16	8.7	9.3	1	9/16	9/16	9/16	10.5	11.4
1 1/8	5/8	1 1/16	5/8	8.6	9.1	1 1/8	5/8	21/32	5/8	10.4	11.1
1 5/8	3/4	3 1/2	3/4	8.4	8.8	1 1/4	3/4	3 1/2	3/4	10.1	10.7
1 5/8	7/8	7/8	7/8	8.3	8.7	1 3/8	7/8	7/8	7/8	9.9	10.5
1 3/4	1	1	1	8.3	8.7	1 3/4	1	1	1	9.8	10.4
2	1 1/8	1 1/8	1 1/8	8.3	8.7	2	1 1/8	1 1/8	1 1/8	9.8	10.4
2 1/4	1 1/4	1 5/16	1 1/4	8.4	8.8	2 1/4	1 1/4	1 5/16	1 1/4	9.9	10.5
2 1/2	1 3/8	1 7/16	1 3/8	8.5	9.0	2 1/2	1 3/8	1 7/16	1 3/8	10.0	10.7
2 1/2	1 1/2	1 9/16	1 1/2	8.8	9.4	2 1/2	1 1/2	1 9/16	1 1/2	10.3	11.1

Hot-Pressed Square Nuts.

For Steamboat Stirrup Bolts.

Short Diameter	Thickness	Hole	Size of Bolt	Price per lb. Blank	Price per lb. Tapped
1 1/2	5/8	7/8	5/8	8.6	9.1
1 3/4	3/4	7/8	5/8	8.6	9.1
1 3/4	3/4	13/16	3/4	8.6	9.0
2	3/4	13/16	3/4	8.6	9.0
2	7/8	13/16	3/4	8.6	9.0

For less than keg lots (200 pounds) of a size the following extras will be charged, viz. :

At the rate of 20 cents per 100 pounds for 100 pounds or more.

At the rate of 50 cents per 100 pounds for less than 100 pounds.

Standard sizes of nuts can always be shipped much more promptly and at a less price than irregular or odd sizes.

Approximate Weight of 1000 Nuts.

UNITED STATES STANDARD SIZES			MANUFACTURERS' STANDARD SIZES				
Dimensions	Square	Hexagon	Dimensions			Square	Hexagon
	Lbs.	Lbs.	Short Dia.	Thickness	Hole	Lbs.	Lbs.
For 1/4 in. Bolt	13 1/2	11	1/2	1/4	7/32	13 1/2	11
" 5/16 "	25	21	5/8	5/16	9/32	25	21
" 3/8 "	36 1/2	30 1/2	3/4	3/8	11/32	46 1/2	38
" 7/16 "	59	49	7/8	7/16	13/32	75	62 1/2
" 1/2 "	79	72	1	1/2	7/16	111 1/2	93
" 9/16 "	109	92 1/2	1 1/8	9/16	1/2	146 1/2	122
" 5/8 "	146	128	1 1/8	5/8	9/16	173 1/2	144 1/2
" 3/4 "	245	216	1 1/4	5/8	9/16	218	182
" 7/8 "	374	316	1 3/8	3/4	21/32	311 1/2	259 1/2
" 1 "	525	462	1 1/2	3/4	21/32	397	331
" 1 1/8 "	747	685	1 5/8	7/8	25/32	507 1/2	423 1/2
" 1 1/4 "	1,017	870	1 3/4	7/8	25/32	609 1/2	. .
" 1 3/8 "	1,400	1,204	1 3/4	1	7/8	637	532
" 1 1/2 "	1,670	1,539	2	1	7/8	884	. .
" 1 5/8 "	2,180	1,923	2	1 1/8	15/16	952	885
" 1 3/4 "	2,625	2,380	2 1/4	1 1/8	15/16	1,282	. .
" 1 7/8 "	3,280	2,857	2 1/4	1 1/4	1 1/16	1,370	1,250
" 2 "	3,820	3,450	2 1/2	1 1/4	1 1/16	1,886	. .
" 2 1/8 "	4,878	3,846	2 3/4	1 3/8	1 3/16	2,439	. .
" 2 1/4 "	5,882	4,348	2 1/2	1 1/2	1 3/16	. .	1,818
" 2 3/8 "	7,143	5,263	2 3/4	1 5/8	1 3/16	. .	2,381
" 2 1/2 "	8,333	6,452	3	1 1/2	1 5/16	3,226	. .
. .	. .	. .	3	1 3/4	1 7/16	. .	3,030
. .	. .	. .	3 1/4	1 5/8	1 7/16	4,166	. .
. .	. .	. .	3 1/4	1 7/8	1 9/16	. .	3,846
. .	. .	. .	3 1/2	1 3/4	1 9/16	4,762	.
. .	. .	. .	3 3/4	1 7/8	1 11/16	5,882	. .
. .	. .	. .	3 1/2	2	1 13/16	. .	4,545
. .	. .	. .	4	2	1 13/16	7,097	. .

Finished Case-Hardened and Semi-Finished Hexagon Nuts.

Fig. 48.

Fig. 49.

The thread and outside of each Finished Nut (Fig. 48) are made to an accurate gauge, and to the standard adopted by the U. S. Government.

The Semi-Finished Nuts (Fig. 49) are the regular Cold-Punched, Chamfered and Trimmed U. S. Standard Hexagon Nuts, tapped and faced true on the bottom.

List Prices of June 1, 1899.

For Bolt	Width	Thickness	Number of Threads	Finished Case-Hardened Nuts, Price, each		Semi-Finished Nuts, Price, each	
				Regular	Double Chamfer	Regular	Double Chamfer
$\frac{1}{4}$ inch	$\frac{1}{2}$	$\frac{1}{4}$	20	.06	.065	.02	.025
$\frac{5}{16}$ "	$\frac{9}{16}$	$\frac{5}{16}$	18	.07	.075	.025	.0275
$\frac{3}{8}$ "	$\frac{11}{16}$	$\frac{3}{8}$	16	.08	.0875	.0325	.04
$\frac{7}{16}$ "	$\frac{25}{32}$	$\frac{7}{16}$	14	.09	.10	.0375	.0475
$\frac{1}{2}$ "	$\frac{7}{8}$	$\frac{1}{2}$	13 (or 12)	.10	.11	.04	.05
$\frac{9}{16}$ "	$\frac{31}{32}$	$\frac{9}{16}$	12	.12	.13	.05	.06
$\frac{5}{8}$ "	$1\frac{1}{16}$	$\frac{5}{8}$	11	.15	.165	.06	.075
$\frac{11}{16}$ "	$1\frac{5}{32}$	$\frac{11}{16}$	11	.20	.22	.085	.105
$\frac{3}{4}$ "	$1\frac{1}{4}$	$\frac{3}{4}$	10	.20	.22	.085	.105
$\frac{7}{8}$ "	$1\frac{7}{16}$	$\frac{7}{8}$	9	.25	.275	.11	.135
1 "	$1\frac{5}{8}$	1	8	.35	.385	.15	.185
$1\frac{1}{8}$ "	$1\frac{13}{16}$	$1\frac{1}{8}$	7	.45	.495	.20	.245
$1\frac{1}{4}$ "	2	$1\frac{1}{4}$	7	.60	.66	.27	.33
$1\frac{3}{8}$ "	$2\frac{3}{16}$	$1\frac{3}{8}$	6	.75	.82	.39	.465
$1\frac{1}{2}$ "	$2\frac{3}{8}$	$1\frac{1}{2}$	6	.95	1.05	.55	.64
$1\frac{5}{8}$ "	$2\frac{9}{16}$	$1\frac{5}{8}$	$5\frac{1}{2}$	1.25	1.38	.72	.835
$1\frac{3}{4}$ "	$2\frac{3}{4}$	$1\frac{3}{4}$	5	1.55	1.70	1.05	1.19
$1\frac{1}{2}$ "	$2\frac{15}{16}$	$1\frac{7}{8}$	5	2.10	2.30	1.30	1.48
2 "	$3\frac{1}{2}$	2	$4\frac{1}{2}$	2.75	3.00	1.60	1.82
$2\frac{1}{4}$ "	$3\frac{1}{2}$	$2\frac{1}{4}$	$4\frac{1}{2}$	5.00	5.50	2.35	2.65
$2\frac{1}{2}$ "	$3\frac{7}{8}$	$2\frac{1}{2}$	4	8.50	9.50	3.75	4.15

For Semi-Finished Nuts, case-hardened, 20 per cent. extra will be charged. Double Chamfered list will be used if Nuts must be rounded on top.

Finished Nuts, not case-hardened, will be charged at same list as Finished Case-Hardened Nuts.

Nut Taps.

UNITED STATES STANDARD SIZES.

For use in regular Nut Tapping Machines.

Fig. 50.

Bolt	Diam. of Shank	Length of Shank	Length of Thread	Total Length of Tap	Size of Hole	Threads per Inch	Price
$\frac{1}{4}$	$\frac{7}{16}$	3	2	8	$\frac{17}{64}$	20	.51
$\frac{5}{16}$	$\frac{1}{4}$	$3\frac{1}{2}$	$2\frac{1}{2}$	8	$\frac{1}{4}$	18	.60
$\frac{3}{8}$	$\frac{17}{64}$	$4\frac{1}{2}$	$2\frac{1}{2}$	10	$\frac{21}{64}$	16	.68
$\frac{7}{16}$	$1\frac{1}{4}$	$4\frac{3}{4}$	$2\frac{3}{4}$	10	$\frac{1}{2}$	14	.77
$\frac{1}{2}$	$2\frac{3}{4}$	$4\frac{3}{4}$	$3\frac{1}{4}$	10	$\frac{25}{64}$	13	.85
$\frac{9}{16}$	$2\frac{3}{4}$	$4\frac{3}{4}$	$3\frac{1}{4}$	12	$\frac{29}{64}$	12	.98
$\frac{5}{8}$	$\frac{1}{2}$	6	$3\frac{1}{2}$	12	$\frac{33}{64}$	11	1.10
$\frac{11}{16}$	$\frac{9}{16}$	6	$3\frac{1}{2}$	12	$\frac{37}{64}$	11	1.23
$\frac{3}{4}$	$\frac{23}{64}$	6	$4\frac{1}{2}$	13	$\frac{5}{8}$	10	1.36
$\frac{7}{8}$	$\frac{23}{32}$	$6\frac{1}{2}$	$4\frac{1}{2}$	14	$\frac{45}{64}$	9	1.80
1	$\frac{53}{64}$	7	5	14	$\frac{25}{32}$	8	2.38
$1\frac{1}{8}$	$1\frac{1}{64}$	$7\frac{1}{2}$	$5\frac{1}{2}$	14	$1\frac{1}{16}$	7	2.72
$1\frac{1}{4}$	$1\frac{5}{64}$	8	6	14	$1\frac{7}{16}$	7	3.15
$1\frac{3}{8}$	$1\frac{11}{64}$	8	7	14	$1\frac{9}{32}$	6	3.57
$1\frac{1}{2}$	$1\frac{11}{32}$	8	7	14	$1\frac{9}{32}$	6	4.00
$1\frac{5}{8}$	$1\frac{3}{8}$	$8\frac{3}{4}$	$7\frac{1}{2}$	. .	$1\frac{3}{8}$	$5\frac{1}{2}$	4.50
$1\frac{3}{4}$	$1\frac{11}{32}$	$9\frac{1}{2}$	$7\frac{1}{2}$	. .	$1\frac{1}{2}$	5	5.10
$1\frac{7}{8}$	$1\frac{17}{32}$	$10\frac{1}{4}$	$7\frac{3}{4}$	. .	$1\frac{5}{8}$	5	5.78
2	$1\frac{11}{16}$	11	8	. .	$1\frac{23}{32}$	$4\frac{1}{2}$	6.55
$2\frac{1}{8}$	$1\frac{13}{16}$	11	8	. .	$1\frac{13}{16}$	$4\frac{1}{2}$	9.00
$2\frac{1}{4}$	$1\frac{15}{16}$	$11\frac{1}{2}$	$8\frac{1}{4}$	. .	$1\frac{15}{16}$	$4\frac{1}{2}$	10.20
$2\frac{3}{8}$	$2\frac{1}{32}$	$11\frac{1}{2}$	$8\frac{1}{4}$	. .	$2\frac{1}{16}$	4	11.50
$2\frac{1}{2}$	$2\frac{5}{32}$	$10\frac{7}{8}$	$9\frac{1}{2}$	. .	$2\frac{3}{16}$	4	12.50
$2\frac{5}{8}$	$2\frac{9}{32}$	$10\frac{7}{8}$	$9\frac{1}{2}$	. .	$2\frac{5}{16}$	4	15.00
$2\frac{3}{4}$	$2\frac{11}{32}$	$10\frac{1}{4}$	$9\frac{3}{4}$	. .	$2\frac{7}{16}$	4	15.00
3	$2\frac{9}{16}$	$10\frac{1}{4}$	$10\frac{3}{4}$	. .	$2\frac{11}{16}$	$3\frac{1}{2}$	18.00

Taps with Left Hand Thread, special prices.
The Points of Taps should enter the Thickness of the Nut.
Special care should be given to keeping Taps sharp.

For Taps longer than above, the following additional prices per Inch of Length will be added to the list prices of Taps as above stated.

Diam. of Tap	Price per additional Inch of Length	Diam. of Tap	Price per additional Inch of Length	Diam. of Tap	Price per additional Inch of Length
$\frac{1}{4}$	5	$\frac{1}{2}$	8	1	12
$\frac{5}{16}$	5	$\frac{5}{8}$	9	$1\frac{1}{4}$	15
$\frac{3}{8}$	6	$\frac{3}{4}$	10	$1\frac{1}{4}$	20
$\frac{7}{16}$	7	$\frac{7}{8}$	11	$1\frac{1}{2}$	25

Galvanized Cross Arm Braces, Brace Bolts, Washers, Fetter Drive Lag Screws, Pole Steps, Cross Arm Bolts, Guy Rods and Guy Clamps, for

Telegraph and Telephone Line Construction.

Complete Line Carried in Stock at Works.

Fig. 51. $1\frac{1}{4} \times \frac{1}{4} \times 28$.

Galvanized Cross Arm Braces.

Fig. 52. $\frac{3}{8} \times 4$

Galvanized Carriage (Brace) Bolt.

Fig. 53. $1\frac{3}{4}$ or $1\frac{1}{2} \times \frac{1}{4}$.

Galvanized Washer for Carriage Bolt.

Fig. 54.

Fetter Drive Thread. $\frac{1}{2} \times 4$ to 7.

Galvanized Lag Screw.

Approximate weight of above given on page 42.

Fig. 55.

Fetter Drive Thread. $\frac{1}{2} \times 8$, 9 and 10.

Galvanized Pole Steps.

Fig. 56. $\frac{3}{8} \times 10$ to 20.

Galvanized Cross Arm Bolts.

Fig. 57.

$2\frac{1}{4} \times 2\frac{1}{4} \times \frac{3}{16}$ for Cross Arm Bolts and Guy Rods.

Galvanized Square Washers.

Fig. 68.

$\frac{5}{8} \times 5$, 6 or 8 feet (furnished with Thimbles, if desired.)

Galvanized Guy Rods.

Approximate weight of above given on page 42.

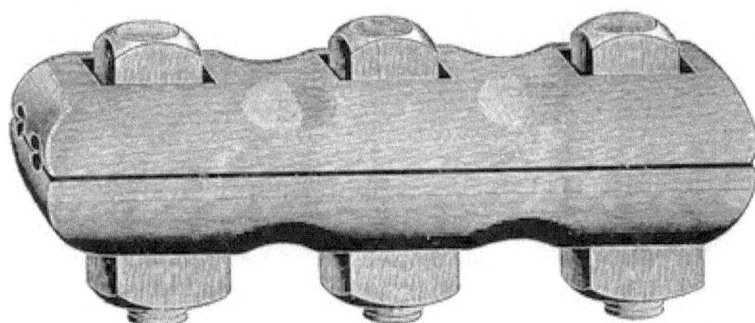

Fig. 59.

Galvanized Three-Bolt Malleable Iron Guy Clamps.

Galvanized Two-Bolt Malleable Iron Guy Clamps also carried in stock.

Weight of Galvanized Material.

Average Weight per Hundred.

Cross Arm Braces, $1\frac{1}{4} \times \frac{1}{4} \times 28$, ...	240	lbs.
Carriage Bolts, $\frac{3}{8} \times 4$, ...	16	"
Round Washers, $1\frac{3}{8} \times \frac{1}{8} \times \frac{9}{32}$, ...	$3\frac{1}{2}$	"
Fetter Drive Lag Screws, $\frac{1}{2} \times 4$, ...	25	"
" " " " 7, ...	40	"
" " " " 7 with washers, ...	$43\frac{1}{2}$	"
Pole Steps, $\frac{5}{8} \times 8$, ...	71	"
" " 9, ...	80	"
" " 10, ...	89	"
Cross Arm Bolts, with Nuts, $\frac{5}{8} \times 10$, 4 in. thread, ...	106	"
" " " " " 12, ...	123	"
" " " " " 14, ...	140	"
" " " " " 16, ...	157	"
Square Washers, $2\frac{1}{4} \times 2\frac{1}{4} \times \frac{3}{16}$, (for Cross Arm Bolts and Guy Rods), . . .	24	"
Guy Rods, $\frac{5}{8} \times 5$ feet, ...	600	"
" " 6 "	695	"
" " 8 "	890	"
Three-Bolt Malleable Iron Guy Clamps, ...	245	"
Two-Bolt Malleable Iron Guy Clamps, ...	105	"

Sizes noted above carried in stock.

Special sizes made promptly to order.

This material is made to conform to the specifications and drawings of the large Telephone and Telegraph Companies.

Material and galvanizing is carefully inspected at Factory.

Fig. 60.

Manufacturers' Standard List of

Plate Washers.

Revised October 9, 1895.   Taking effect October 10, 1895.

Diameter	Size of Hole	Thickness Wire Gauge	Size of Bolt	Price per Pound	Average Number in 100 lbs.
$\frac{7}{8}$	$\frac{1}{4}$	No. 18	$\frac{3}{16}$	14.00	44,075
$\frac{3}{4}$	$\frac{5}{16}$	" 16	$\frac{1}{4}$	12.20	13,845
$\frac{7}{8}$	$\frac{3}{8}$	" 16	$\frac{5}{16}$	11.40	11,220
1	$\frac{7}{16}$	" 14	$\frac{3}{8}$	10.50	6,573
$1\frac{1}{8}$	$\frac{1}{2}$	" 14	$\frac{7}{16}$	9.70	4,261
$1\frac{1}{4}$	$\frac{9}{16}$	" 12	$\frac{1}{2}$	9.20	2,683
$1\frac{3}{8}$	$\frac{5}{8}$	" 12	$\frac{9}{16}$	9.10	2,249
$1\frac{1}{2}$	$\frac{11}{16}$	" 10	$\frac{5}{8}$	9.00	1,315
2	$1\frac{3}{16}$	" 10	$\frac{3}{4}$	8.80	1,013
$2\frac{1}{4}$	$1\frac{1}{16}$	" 9	$\frac{7}{8}$	8.80	858
$2\frac{1}{2}$	$1\frac{3}{16}$	" 9	1	8.80	617
$2\frac{3}{4}$	$1\frac{1}{4}$	" 9	$1\frac{1}{8}$	8.80	516
3	$1\frac{3}{8}$	" 9	$1\frac{1}{4}$	9.00	403
$3\frac{1}{4}$	$1\frac{1}{2}$	" 8	$1\frac{3}{8}$	9.00	320
$3\frac{1}{2}$	$1\frac{5}{8}$	" 8	$1\frac{1}{2}$	9.20	278
$3\frac{3}{4}$	$1\frac{3}{4}$	" 8	$1\frac{5}{8}$	9.20	247
4	$1\frac{7}{8}$	" 8	$1\frac{3}{4}$	9.50	224
$4\frac{1}{4}$	2	" 8	$1\frac{7}{8}$	9.50	200
$4\frac{1}{2}$	$2\frac{1}{8}$	" 8	2	9.50	180

Fig. 61.

Square Washers.

STANDARD SIZES.

Wide	Thick	Hole	Bolt	Number in 100 lbs.
$1\frac{1}{4}$	$\frac{1}{8}$	$\frac{7}{16}$	$\frac{3}{8}$	1,300
$1\frac{3}{4}$	$\frac{1}{8}$	$\frac{1}{2}$	$\frac{7}{16}$	1,100
2	$\frac{3}{16}$	$\frac{9}{16}$	$\frac{1}{2}$	500
$2\frac{1}{4}$	$\frac{1}{4}$	$\frac{5}{8}$	$\frac{5}{8}$	315
$2\frac{1}{2}$	$\frac{1}{4}$	$\frac{3}{4}$	$\frac{3}{4}$	250
3	$\frac{1}{4}$	$\frac{7}{8}$	$\frac{7}{8}$	165
$3\frac{1}{2}$	$\frac{5}{16}$	$1\frac{1}{16}$	1	87
4	$\frac{3}{8}$	$1\frac{1}{8}$	$1\frac{1}{8}$	65
$4\frac{1}{2}$	$\frac{3}{8}$	$1\frac{3}{8}$	$1\frac{1}{4}$	48
5	$\frac{3}{8}$	$1\frac{1}{2}$	$1\frac{3}{8}$	40
6	$\frac{3}{8}$	$1\frac{5}{8}$	$1\frac{1}{2}$	28

Prices of Square Washers depend very much upon quantity wanted, as they are made up specially to order.   Lowest figures will be quoted on application.

Pressed Wrought Iron Turnbuckles.

Fig. 62.

PRICE LIST.

Diameter of Stub Ends	Inside Opening of Buckle	Outside Length of Buckle	Total Length of Buckle with Stub Ends in	Price
3/8 inch.	4 1/2 inches.	6 1/2 inches.	17 inches.	.40 each.
7/16 "	4 3/4 "	6 3/4 "	17 "	.42 "
1/2 "	6 "	8 "	21 "	.45 "
5/8 "	6 "	8 1/4 "	23 "	.50 "
3/4 "	6 "	8 1/2 "	23 "	.63 "
7/8 "	6 "	9 "	23 "	.75 "
1 "	6 "	9 "	23 "	.88 "
1 1/8 "	6 "	9 1/4 "	23 "	1.00 "
1 1/4 "	6 "	9 1/4 "	23 "	1.25 "
1 3/8 "	6 "	9 1/4 "	23 "	1.38 "
1 1/2 "	6 1/2 "	10 1/2 "	25 "	1.50 "
1 3/4 "	6 1/2 "	11 1/2 "	26 "	2.00 "

Longer Turnbuckles are made to order at special prices.
Turnbuckles with swivel in one end furnished to order.

Cast Iron Washers and Spools.

Made by our own Foundry.

WEIGHT AND SIZE OF CAST WASHERS.

Weight per Hundred.

Size of Bolt or Rod	Round Washers Dimensions	Round Washers Weight	Diamond Washers Weight	Diamond Washers Thickness in Centre	Diamond Washers Width and Length
inch	inch	lbs.	lbs.	inch	inch
3/8	1 1/2 × 7/16	9 1/2	. . .	. . .	. . .
1/2	2 × 3/8	21	. . .	. . .	. . .
5/8	2 1/2 × 1/2	43	215	3/4	4 1/2 × 8
3/4	3 × 5/8	70	438	1	5 1/2 ×10
7/8	3 1/2× 3/4	113	750	1 1/16	7 ×12
1	4 × 7/8	175	1,300	1 7/16	8 ×14
1 1/8	4 1/2×1	256	1,860	1 1/8	9 1/4×16
1 1/4	5 ×1 1/4	332	1,860	1 3/4	9 1/2×16
1 3/8	5 1/2×1 1/4	455	2,800	2 1/4	10 1/2×18
1 1/2	6 ×1 3/8	610	2,800	2 1/2	10 1/2×18
1 3/4	7 ×1 1/2	865	. . .	. . .	. . .
2	7 1/2×1 5/8	1,115	. . .	. . .	. . .

Special Washers and Spools made according to drawing or sample.
Net prices upon receipt of specifications.

Pipe Sleeve Nuts.

With Right and Left-Hand U. S. Threads and Stub Ends,

Fig. 63.

Diameter of Screw	Length of Pipe Sleeve Nut	Outside Diameter of Pipe	Length of Hexagon Sleeve Nut	List Price Each
$\frac{3}{8}$	5	.840	3	.60
$\frac{1}{2}$	$5\frac{1}{2}$	1.050	3	.80
$\frac{5}{8}$	7	1.315	$3\frac{1}{2}$	1.00
$\frac{3}{4}$	7	1.315	4	1.25
$\frac{7}{8}$	8	1.660	$4\frac{1}{2}$	1.50
1	$9\frac{1}{2}$	1.900	5	2.00
$1\frac{1}{8}$	$9\frac{1}{2}$	1.900	$5\frac{1}{2}$	2.50
$1\frac{1}{4}$	$11\frac{1}{2}$	2.375	6	3.00
$1\frac{3}{8}$	$11\frac{1}{2}$	2.375	$6\frac{1}{2}$	3.50
$1\frac{1}{2}$	$13\frac{1}{2}$	2.875	7	4.00
$1\frac{5}{8}$	$13\frac{1}{2}$	2.875	$7\frac{1}{2}$	4.50
$1\frac{3}{4}$	$13\frac{1}{2}$	2.875	8	5.00
$1\frac{7}{8}$	15	3.500	8	5.50
2	15	3.500	$8\frac{1}{2}$	6.00

Hexagon Sleeve Nuts.

With Right and Left-Hand U. S. Threads and Stub Ends.

Fig. 64.

Sold at List Prices above.

Railroad Spikes with Pressed or Rolled Points.

Fig. 65.

FOR STEAM AND ELECTRIC RAILWAYS.

Prices Quoted on Application.

Spikes in One Mile of Single Track.

Size	With Ties 2 feet between centres, 4 Spikes to a Tie	Average number in Keg, 200 lbs.
6 × $1\frac{9}{16}$	6600 lbs. or 33 kegs	320
$5\frac{1}{2}$ × $1\frac{9}{16}$	6212 " 31 "	340
5 × $1\frac{9}{16}$	5863 " $29\frac{1}{3}$ "	360
6 × $\frac{1}{2}$	5028 " $25\frac{1}{4}$ "	420
$5\frac{1}{2}$ × $\frac{1}{2}$	4641 " $23\frac{1}{4}$ "	455
5 × $\frac{1}{2}$	4267 " $21\frac{1}{3}$ "	495
$4\frac{1}{2}$ × $\frac{1}{2}$	3911 " $19\frac{1}{2}$ "	540
4 × $\frac{1}{2}$	3520 " $17\frac{3}{5}$ "	600
5 × $1\frac{7}{16}$	3520 " $17\frac{3}{5}$ "	600
$4\frac{1}{2}$ × $1\frac{7}{16}$	3224 " $16\frac{1}{8}$ "	655
4 × $1\frac{7}{16}$	2933 " $14\frac{3}{4}$ "	720
$3\frac{1}{2}$ × $1\frac{7}{16}$	2600 " 13 "	810
5 × $\frac{3}{8}$	2576 " 13 "	820
$4\frac{1}{2}$ × $\frac{3}{8}$	2347 " $11\frac{3}{4}$ "	900
4 × $\frac{3}{8}$	2112 " $10\frac{1}{2}$ "	1000
$3\frac{1}{2}$ × $\frac{3}{8}$	1885 " $9\frac{1}{2}$ "	1120
3 × $\frac{3}{8}$	1656 " $8\frac{1}{4}$ "	1275
$2\frac{1}{2}$ × $\frac{3}{8}$	1426 " $7\frac{1}{8}$ "	1480

Dock or Wharf Spikes.

ROUND OR SQUARE.

Made of Iron or Steel, with Head and Point as specified.

Average Weight per 100.

Size	½ in. Square	⅝ in. Square	¾ in. Square	⅞ in. Square	1 in. Square
6 inches	51	. .	. .	. .	. .
8 "	64	. .	. .	. .	. .
10 "	78	121	171	238	. .
11 "	85	132	187	260	. .
12 "	92	143	203	281	388
13 "	99	154	219	303	416
14 "	106	165	234	324	444
15 "	113	176	250	346	472
16 "	120	187	266	367	500
17 "	. .	198	282	389	528
18 "	. .	209	298	411	558
19 "	. .	220	314	432	586
20 "	. .	231	329	454	614
22 "	. .	. .	360	497	670
24 "	. .	. .	390	540	726
26 "	. .	. .	420	584	782

Forgings, Plates and Rods.

We are prepared to furnish promptly the Wrought and Cast Iron Work for Dock,
Bridge, Roof and Floor Construction, and will name prices on this
class of work upon receipt of specifications.

Manufacturers' Standard List of

Bridge and Roof Bolts.

Fig. 66.

Price per Pound, with Square Head on One End and Square Nut on the other, or
Square Nut on Each End, as Preferred.

Adopted January 30, 1895, to take effect February 20, 1895.

Length	⅞ Diam.	⅞ to 1¼ Diam.	1¼ to 1¼ Diam.	1⅝ to 2 Diam.
30 inches to 4 feet	.09.2	.08.8	.09.2	.10.0
4 feet to 8 "	.08.8	.08.4	.08.8	.09.4
8 " to 12 "	.08.4	.08.0	.08.4	.08.8
12 " to 20 "	.08.0	.07.6	.08.0	.08.4

We make the usual forgings accompanying structural bolts, such as stirrups
and hanger bolts, with the necessary wrought or cast washers; also bolts with
countersunk heads to fit into cast header washers, as shown in cut below. Illus-
trations of structural forgings are shown among the cuts in the latter part of the
catalogue.

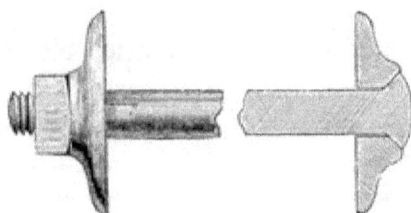

Fig. 67.

Bridge and Roof Bolts.

Price per Pound, with Both Ends Upset and Fitted with Hexagon Nuts.

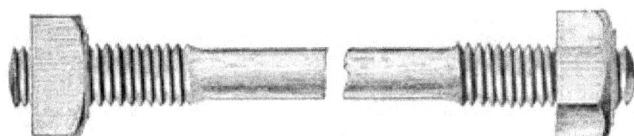

Fig. 68.

Price per Pound, in cents.

Adopted January 30, 1895, to take effect February 20, 1895.

Length	¾ to 1¼ Diam.	1¼ to 1½ Diam.	1½ to 2 Diam.	2¼ to 3 Diam.
4 to 8 feet	.12.0	.12.4	.13.2	.14.4
8 to 12 "	.11.0	.11.4	.12.2	.13.2
12 to 16 "	.10.0	.10.4	.11.2	.12.4
16 to 20 "	.09.2	.09.6	.10.4	.11.6

Dimensions of Upset Ends on Round Iron.

Diam. of Bar	Diam. of Upset	Length of Upset	Threads per Inch	Diam. of Bar	Diam. of Upset	Length of Upset	Threads per Inch
¾	1	2¾	8	1¾	2⅛	5½	4½
⅞	1⅛	3	7	1⅞	2¼	5¾	4½
1	1¼	3¼	7	2	2⅜	6	4
1⅛	1⅜	3½	6	2⅛	2½	6½	4
1¼	1½	4	6	2¼	2⅝	6¾	4
1⅜	1¾	4½	5	2⅜	2¾	7	4
1½	1⅞	5	5	2½	2⅞	7½	3½
1⅝	2	5¼	4½	2⅝	3	8	3½

We are prepared to make Upset Rods up to 3 inch diameter from best refined iron.

Merchant Iron and Steel.

This company has extensive plants for the manufacture of iron and steel, embracing three establishments in Lebanon, and one in Reading, Pa. We have an annual capacity of about 150,000 tons. Our facilities include thirty-one puddling furnaces, twenty heating furnaces and eighteen trains of rolls, three of which are twenty inch muck bar trains and fifteen finishing trains, the latter as follows : Two 18 inch, one 16 inch, four 12 inch, four 10 inch, one 9 inch and three 8 inch.

We manufacture common and refined bars in all grades to suit the requirements of our customers, and in addition, the highest grade of iron for boiler stay bolts and for other exacting purposes ; also Bessemer and Open Hearth steel bars and rods within practicable limits as to chemical and physical specifications.

While we consume the greater part of our production of rolled iron and steel in our own manufactures, yet with the improvements in progress and others contemplated, we hope to have a considerable surplus to offer to the general trade, and we, therefore, solicit inquiries.

Sizes of Bar Iron Rolled by

AMERICAN IRON AND STEEL MANUFACTURING CO.

ROUNDS.

$\frac{1}{4}$	$\frac{9}{32}$	$\frac{5}{16}$	$\frac{11}{32}$	$\frac{3}{8}$	$\frac{13}{32}$	$\frac{7}{16}$	$\frac{15}{32}$	$\frac{1}{2}$	$\frac{17}{32}$	$\frac{9}{16}$	$\frac{19}{32}$	$\frac{5}{8}$
$\frac{21}{32}$	$\frac{11}{16}$	$\frac{23}{32}$	$\frac{3}{4}$	$\frac{25}{32}$	$\frac{13}{16}$	$\frac{27}{32}$	$\frac{7}{8}$	$\frac{29}{32}$	$\frac{15}{16}$	1	$1\frac{1}{32}$	$1\frac{1}{16}$
$1\frac{3}{32}$	$1\frac{1}{8}$	$1\frac{5}{32}$	$1\frac{3}{16}$	$1\frac{1}{4}$	$1\frac{9}{32}$	$1\frac{5}{16}$	$1\frac{3}{8}$	$1\frac{7}{16}$	$1\frac{1}{2}$	$1\frac{9}{16}$	$1\frac{5}{8}$	$1\frac{11}{16}$
$1\frac{3}{4}$	$1\frac{7}{8}$	2	$2\frac{1}{8}$	$2\frac{1}{4}$	$2\frac{3}{8}$	$2\frac{1}{2}$	$2\frac{5}{8}$	$2\frac{3}{4}$	$2\frac{7}{8}$	3	$3\frac{1}{8}$	$3\frac{1}{4}$
$3\frac{3}{8}$	$3\frac{1}{2}$	$3\frac{5}{8}$	$3\frac{3}{4}$	$3\frac{7}{8}$	4	$4\frac{1}{4}$	$4\frac{1}{2}$	$4\frac{3}{4}$	5	$5\frac{1}{4}$	$5\frac{1}{2}$	

SQUARES.

$\frac{1}{4}$	$\frac{9}{32}$	$\frac{5}{16}$	$\frac{3}{8}$	$\frac{7}{16}$	$\frac{15}{32}$	$\frac{1}{2}$	$\frac{17}{32}$	$\frac{9}{16}$	$\frac{19}{32}$	$\frac{5}{8}$	$\frac{11}{16}$
$\frac{3}{4}$	$\frac{13}{16}$	$\frac{7}{8}$	1	$1\frac{1}{8}$	$1\frac{1}{4}$	$1\frac{3}{8}$	$1\frac{1}{2}$	$1\frac{5}{8}$	$1\frac{3}{4}$	$1\frac{7}{8}$	2
$2\frac{1}{8}$	$2\frac{1}{4}$	$2\frac{3}{8}$	$2\frac{1}{2}$	$2\frac{5}{8}$	3	$3\frac{1}{4}$	$3\frac{1}{2}$	$3\frac{3}{4}$	4	$4\frac{1}{4}$	$4\frac{1}{2}$

HALF OVALS.

$\frac{1}{2}\times\frac{9}{16}$	$\frac{9}{16}\times\frac{7}{16}$	$\frac{5}{8}\times\frac{7}{16}$	$\frac{3}{8}\times\frac{1}{4}$	$\frac{3}{4}\times\frac{7}{16}$	$\frac{3}{4}\times\frac{9}{32}$	$\frac{7}{8}\times\frac{1}{4}$	$\frac{7}{8}\times\frac{7}{16}$
$\frac{7}{8}\times\frac{7}{32}$	$\frac{7}{8}\times\frac{1}{4}$	$1\times\frac{9}{16}$	$1\times\frac{1}{4}$	$1\times\frac{9}{16}$	$1\times\frac{3}{8}$	$1\frac{1}{8}\times\frac{1}{4}$	$1\frac{1}{8}\times\frac{9}{32}$
$1\frac{1}{8}\times\frac{3}{8}$	$1\frac{1}{8}\times\frac{7}{16}$	$1\frac{1}{4}\times\frac{7}{16}$	$1\frac{1}{4}\times\frac{3}{8}$	$1\frac{1}{4}\times\frac{7}{16}$	$1\frac{3}{8}\times\frac{3}{8}$	$1\frac{1}{2}\times\frac{3}{8}$	$1\frac{1}{4}\times\frac{1}{2}$

$$2\times\frac{1}{4}$$

HALF ROUNDS.

$\frac{3}{8}$	$\frac{7}{16}$	$\frac{1}{2}$	$\frac{5}{8}$	$\frac{11}{16}$	$\frac{3}{4}$	$\frac{13}{16}$	$\frac{7}{8}$	1	$1\frac{1}{8}$	$1\frac{1}{4}$	$1\frac{5}{16}$

GROOVED OR CHANNEL IRON.

$$\tfrac{3}{4}\times\tfrac{1}{2} \quad \tfrac{3}{4}\times\tfrac{1}{2} \quad \tfrac{7}{8}\times\tfrac{1}{2} \quad 1\times\tfrac{1}{2}$$

Sizes of Bar Iron

Rolled by

AMERICAN IRON AND STEEL MANUFACTURING CO.

FLATS.

$\frac{1}{2}\frac{3}{8}\times\frac{9}{16}$ to $\frac{3}{8}$	$1\frac{1}{16}\times\frac{1}{4}$ to $\frac{7}{8}$	$2\frac{3}{8}\times\frac{1}{4}$ to $1\frac{3}{4}$
$\frac{1}{32}\times\frac{9}{16}$ to $\frac{7}{16}$	$1\frac{9}{32}\times\frac{3}{8}$ to 1	$2\frac{7}{16}\times\frac{7}{8}$ to 2
$\frac{7}{16}\times\frac{7}{16}$ to $\frac{3}{8}$	$1\frac{1}{8}\times\frac{1}{8}$ to $\frac{7}{8}$	$2\frac{1}{2}\times\frac{1}{4}$ to 2
$\frac{1}{2}\times\frac{7}{16}$ to $\frac{7}{16}$	$1\frac{9}{16}\times\frac{3}{8}$ to 1	$2\frac{9}{16}\times\frac{1}{8}$ to $2\frac{1}{4}$
$\frac{17}{32}\times\frac{7}{16}$ to $\frac{1}{2}$	$1\frac{1}{4}\times\frac{7}{16}$ to 1	$2\frac{5}{8}\times\frac{1}{4}$ to $2\frac{1}{4}$
$\frac{9}{16}\times\frac{1}{4}$ to $\frac{1}{2}$	$1\frac{5}{16}\times\frac{3}{8}$ to $1\frac{1}{4}$	$2\frac{3}{4}\times\frac{1}{4}$ to 2
$\frac{19}{32}\times\frac{1}{4}$ to $\frac{1}{2}$	$1\frac{1}{2}\times\frac{1}{2}$ to 1	$2\frac{7}{8}\times\frac{5}{8}$ to $2\frac{1}{4}$
$\frac{5}{8}\times\frac{7}{16}$ to $\frac{9}{16}$	$1\frac{3}{8}\times\frac{7}{16}$ to 1	$3\times\frac{1}{4}$ to $2\frac{5}{8}$
$\frac{21}{32}\times\frac{7}{16}$ to $\frac{5}{8}$	$1\frac{13}{32}\times\frac{5}{8}$ to 1	$3\frac{1}{8}\times1\frac{1}{2}$ to $2\frac{5}{8}$
$\frac{11}{16}\times\frac{7}{16}$ to $\frac{5}{8}$	$1\frac{7}{16}\times\frac{3}{8}$ to $1\frac{3}{8}$	$3\frac{1}{4}\times\frac{1}{4}$ to $2\frac{5}{8}$
$\frac{23}{32}\times\frac{7}{16}$ to $\frac{5}{8}$	$1\frac{1}{2}\times\frac{7}{16}$ to $1\frac{1}{4}$	$3\frac{1}{2}\times\frac{1}{4}$ to $2\frac{7}{8}$
$\frac{3}{4}\times\frac{7}{16}$ to $\frac{5}{8}$	$1\frac{9}{16}\times\frac{3}{8}$ to $1\frac{1}{4}$	$3\frac{3}{4}\times\frac{1}{4}$ to $2\frac{3}{4}$
$\frac{25}{32}\times\frac{7}{16}$ to $\frac{5}{8}$	$1\frac{5}{8}\times\frac{1}{4}$ to $1\frac{1}{2}$	$4\times\frac{1}{4}$ to 3
$1\frac{1}{8}\times\frac{3}{8}$ to $\frac{5}{8}$	$1\frac{11}{16}\times\frac{1}{2}$ to $1\frac{1}{2}$	$4\frac{1}{4}\times\frac{1}{4}$ to $1\frac{3}{4}$
$\frac{27}{32}\times\frac{7}{16}$ to $\frac{5}{8}$	$1\frac{3}{4}\times\frac{1}{4}$ to $1\frac{7}{16}$	$4\frac{1}{2}\times\frac{1}{4}$ to 2
$\frac{7}{8}\times\frac{1}{8}$ to $\frac{3}{4}$	$1\frac{13}{16}\times\frac{9}{16}$ to $1\frac{3}{4}$	$4\frac{3}{4}\times\frac{1}{4}$ to 2
$\frac{29}{32}\times\frac{3}{8}$ to $\frac{5}{8}$	$1\frac{7}{8}\times\frac{3}{8}$ to $1\frac{1}{2}$	$5\times\frac{1}{4}$ to 2
$1\frac{1}{16}\times\frac{3}{8}$ to $\frac{7}{8}$	$1\frac{15}{16}\times\frac{1}{2}$ to $1\frac{3}{4}$	$5\frac{1}{2}\times\frac{1}{4}$ to 2
$\frac{31}{16}\times\frac{3}{8}$ to $\frac{15}{16}$	$2\times\frac{1}{4}$ to $1\frac{3}{4}$	$6\times\frac{1}{4}$ to 2
$1\times\frac{1}{8}$ to $\frac{7}{8}$	$2\frac{1}{16}\times1$ to 2	$7\times\frac{1}{4}$ to 2
$1\frac{1}{32}\times\frac{3}{8}$ to 1	$2\frac{1}{8}\times\frac{1}{4}$ to $1\frac{1}{4}$	$8\times\frac{3}{8}$ to 2
	$2\frac{1}{4}\times\frac{1}{4}$ to 2	

We also roll round edge flats, $\frac{3}{8}$ to 5 inches wide, $\frac{1}{4}$ to $1\frac{1}{4}$ thick, as well as nut iron in a great variety of sizes.

National Bar Iron Manufacturers' Schedule of

Minimum Extra Prices above the Base Bar Price, to be Charged for Extra Sizes of Iron.

Adopted March 16, 1899.

ROUNDS AND SQUARES.

$\frac{7}{16}$	$2\frac{4}{10}$ extra
$\frac{7}{32}$	$1\frac{7}{10}$ "
$\frac{1}{4}$ to $\frac{9}{32}$	$\frac{9}{10}$ "
$\frac{7}{16}$ to $\frac{11}{32}$	$\frac{7}{10}$ "
$\frac{3}{8}$ to $\frac{13}{32}$	$\frac{6}{10}$ "
$\frac{7}{16}$ to $\frac{15}{32}$	$\frac{4}{10}$ "
$\frac{1}{2}$ to $\frac{9}{16}$	$\frac{4}{10}$ "
$\frac{5}{8}$ to $\frac{11}{16}$	$\frac{3}{10}$ "
$\frac{3}{4}$ to $\frac{7}{8}$	$\frac{1}{10}$ "
1 to $1\frac{7}{8}$	Base sizes no extra
2 to $2\frac{7}{8}$	$\frac{2}{10}$ extra
3 to $3\frac{1}{2}$	$\frac{7}{10}$ "
$3\frac{5}{8}$ to 4	$\frac{9}{10}$ "
$4\frac{1}{8}$ to $4\frac{1}{2}$	1 c. "
$4\frac{5}{8}$ to 5	$1\frac{3}{10}$ "
$5\frac{1}{8}$ to 6	$1\frac{7}{10}$ "
$6\frac{3}{8}$ to $6\frac{1}{2}$	$2\frac{3}{10}$ "
$6\frac{5}{8}$ to $7\frac{1}{4}$	$2\frac{4}{10}$ "

FLATS.

$\frac{3}{8}$ to $\frac{9}{16} \times \frac{1}{4}$ to $\frac{9}{16}$	$1\frac{4}{10}$ extra
$\frac{1}{2}$ to $\frac{9}{16} \times \frac{1}{4}$ to $\frac{7}{16}$	1 c. "
$\frac{1}{2}$ to $\frac{9}{16} \times \frac{3}{8}$ to $\frac{1}{2}$	$\frac{9}{10}$ "
$\frac{5}{8}$ to $\frac{11}{16} \times \frac{1}{4}$ to $\frac{9}{16}$	$\frac{6}{10}$ "
$\frac{5}{8}$ to $\frac{11}{16} \times \frac{3}{8}$ to $\frac{5}{8}$	$\frac{5}{10}$ "
$\frac{3}{4}$ to $\frac{13}{16} \times \frac{1}{4}$ to $\frac{7}{16}$	$\frac{5}{10}$ "
$\frac{7}{8}$ to $\frac{13}{16} \times \frac{3}{8}$ to $\frac{3}{4}$	$\frac{4}{10}$ "
1 to $1\frac{3}{8} \times \frac{1}{4}$ to $\frac{7}{16}$	$\frac{1}{8}$ "
1 to $1\frac{7}{16} \times \frac{5}{8}$ to $\frac{7}{8}$	$\frac{2}{10}$ "
$1\frac{1}{2}$ to $1\frac{5}{8} \times \frac{3}{4}$ to 1	$\frac{7}{10}$ "

FLATS—Continued.

1½ to 4	× ¼ to 5/16	2/10	extra
1½ to 4	× ⅜ to 1	Base	no extra
1½ to 4	× 1 1/16 to 1½	2/10	"
2 to 4	× 1⅝ to 2	4/10	"
2 to 4	× 2⅛ to 3	6/10	"
4¼ to 6	× ¼ to 5/16	3/10	"
4¼ to 6	× ⅜ to 1	1/10	"
4¼ to 6	× 1 1/16 to 1½	4/10	"
4¼ to 6	× 1⅝ to 2	6/10	"
4¼ to 6	× 2⅛ to 3	8/10	"
6¼ to 6¾	× ¼ to 5/16	5/10	"
7 to 8	× ¼ to 5/16	7/10	"
6¼ to 8	× ⅜ to 1½	6/10	"
6¼ to 8	× 1⅝ to 2	8/10	"
6¼ to 8	× 2⅛ to 3	1c.	"
8¼ to 10	× ¼ to 5/16	7/10	"
8¼ to 10	× ⅜ to 1	4/10	"
8¼ to 10	× 1 1/16 to 1½	8/10	"
8¼ to 10	× 1⅝ to 2	1c.	"

Flats 7/32 thick 1/10 c. per lb. higher than ¼ to 5/16 thick.
Bevel edge Shaft Iron 1/10 c. higher than same size of Flats.
All round edge iron 1/10 c. per lb. extra.
Horse Shoe Iron all sizes 1 c. per lb. extra.

OVAL IRON.

⅜ to 7/16	1 1/10	extra
½ to 9/16	5/10	"
½ to 9/16 × 3/16	1c.	"
⅝ to 11/16	4/10	"
⅝ to 11/16 × ⅛	1 3/10	"
¾ to 13/16	3/10	"
⅞ to 1½	1/10	"

HALF OVAL AND HALF ROUND.

¼	4 5/10	extra
5/16	3 5/10	"
⅜ to 7/16	2 4/10	"
½ to 9/16	1 2/10	"
⅝ to 11/16	3/10	"
¾ to 13/16	1/10	"
⅞ to 2	2/10	"
2⅛ to 3	6/10	"

Half ovals less than ¼ their width in thickness, extra price.

United States Standard Screw Threads and Nuts.

Fig. 69.

Diameter of Screw	Threads per Inch	Diameter at Root of Thread	Short Diameter, Square and Hexagon	Long Diameter, Hexagon	Long Diameter, Square	Thickness
1/4	20	.185	1/2	37/64	7/10	1/4
5/16	18	.240	19/32	11/16	13/16	5/16
3/8	16	.294	11/16	51/64	31/32	3/8
7/16	14	.344	25/32	9/10	1 5/64	7/16
1/2	13	.400	7/8	1	1 15/64	1/2
9/16	12	.454	31/32	1 1/8	1 23/64	9/16
5/8	11	.507	1 1/16	1 7/32	1 1/2	5/8
3/4	10	.620	1 1/4	1 7/16	1 43/64	3/4
7/8	9	.731	1 7/16	1 41/64	2 1/32	7/8
1	8	.837	1 5/8	1 7/8	2 19/64	1
1 1/8	7	.940	1 11/16	2 3/32	2 17/32	1 1/8
1 1/4	7	1.065	2	2 5/16	2 53/64	1 1/4
1 3/8	6	1.160	2 3/16	2 17/32	3 3/32	1 3/8
1 1/2	6	1.284	2 3/8	2 3/4	3 11/32	1 1/2
1 5/8	5 1/2	1.389	2 9/16	2 31/32	3 5/8	1 5/8
1 3/4	5	1.491	2 3/4	3 3/16	3 53/64	1 3/4
1 7/8	5	1.616	2 15/16	3 13/32	4 1/32	1 7/8
2	4 1/2	1.712	3 1/8	3 5/8	4 13/64	2
2 1/4	4 1/2	1.962	3 1/2	4 1/16	4 61/64	2 1/4
2 1/2	4	2.176	3 7/8	4 1/2	5 13/64	2 1/2
2 3/4	4	2.426	4 1/4	4 29/32	6	2 3/4
3	3 1/2	2.629	4 5/8	5 3/8	6 17/32	3
3 1/4	3 1/2	2.879	5	5 13/16	7 1/16	3 1/4
3 1/2	3 1/4	3.100	5 3/8	6 7/64	7 33/64	3 1/2
3 3/4	3	3.317	5 3/4	6 1/2	8 1/8	3 3/4
4	3	3.567	6 1/8	7 3/32	8 41/64	4

All Bolts cut United States Standard Thread, unless otherwise ordered.

V THREAD STANDARD.

Fig. 70.

The V Thread is the oldest style of thread, and is still in use largely in some sections of the United States.

Diameter, . . .	$\frac{1}{4}$	$\frac{5}{16}$	$\frac{3}{8}$	$\frac{7}{16}$	$\frac{1}{2}$	$\frac{9}{16}$	$\frac{5}{8}$	$\frac{11}{16}$	$\frac{3}{4}$	$\frac{13}{16}$
No. of Threads per Inch, . .	20	18	16	14	12	12	11	11	10	10
Diameter, ...	$\frac{7}{8}$	$\frac{15}{16}$	1	$1\frac{1}{8}$	$1\frac{1}{4}$	$1\frac{3}{8}$	$1\frac{1}{2}$	$1\frac{5}{8}$	$1\frac{3}{4}$	
No. of Threads per Inch, . .	9	9	8	7	7	6	6	5	5	

WHITWORTH STANDARD.

Fig. 71.

This standard has been adopted by Great Britain.

Diameter, . . .	$\frac{1}{4}$	$\frac{5}{16}$	$\frac{3}{8}$	$\frac{7}{16}$	$\frac{1}{2}$	$\frac{9}{16}$	$\frac{5}{8}$	$\frac{11}{16}$	$\frac{3}{4}$	$\frac{13}{16}$
No. of Threads per Inch, . .	20	18	16	14	12	12	11	11	10	10
Diameter, ...	$\frac{7}{8}$	$\frac{15}{16}$	1	$1\frac{1}{8}$	$1\frac{1}{4}$	$1\frac{3}{8}$	$1\frac{1}{2}$	$1\frac{5}{8}$	$1\frac{3}{4}$	
No. of Threads per Inch, . .	9	9	8	7	7	6	6	5	5	

COACH AND LAG SCREWS.

Diameter, . . .	$\frac{5}{16}$	$\frac{3}{8}$	$\frac{1}{2}$	$\frac{5}{8}$	$\frac{3}{4}$	$\frac{7}{8}$	1	$1\frac{1}{8}$
No. of Threads per Inch, . .	9	7	5	5	$4\frac{1}{2}$	4	4	3

COACH AND LAG SCREWS OF ALL DIAMETERS WILL BE THREADED TO THE FOLLOWING LENGTHS.

Length of Screw	Length of Thread	Length of Screw	Length of Thread
$1\frac{1}{2}$	1	5	$2\frac{3}{4}$
2	$1\frac{1}{4}$	$5\frac{1}{2}$	3
$2\frac{1}{2}$	$1\frac{1}{2}$	6	$3\frac{1}{4}$
3	$1\frac{3}{4}$	7	$3\frac{3}{4}$
$3\frac{1}{2}$	2	8	$4\frac{1}{4}$
4	$2\frac{1}{4}$	9	$4\frac{3}{4}$
$4\frac{1}{2}$	$2\frac{1}{2}$	10 to 12	5

Manufacturers' Standard

Dimensions of Heads for Bolts.

Diameter Bolt	Square and Hexagon Heads	Button Heads and Carriage Bolt Heads	Tee Heads	Square and Round Countersunk Heads	Forged Set Screw Heads
	Width and Thickness	Width and Thickness	Length, Width and Thickness	Width and Thickness	Width and Thickness
$\frac{1}{4}$	$\frac{3}{8} \times \frac{3}{16}$	$\frac{1}{2} \times \frac{1}{8}$	$\frac{1}{2} \times \frac{1}{4} \times \frac{3}{16}$	$\frac{1}{2} \times \frac{3}{16}$	$\frac{1}{4} \times \frac{1}{4}$
$\frac{5}{16}$	$\frac{1}{2} \times \frac{1}{4}$	$\frac{5}{8} \times \frac{5}{32}$	$\frac{5}{8} \times \frac{5}{16} \times \frac{1}{4}$	$\frac{5}{8} \times \frac{7}{32}$	$\frac{5}{16} \times \frac{5}{16}$
$\frac{3}{8}$	$\frac{9}{16} \times \frac{5}{16}$	$\frac{3}{4} \times \frac{7}{32}$	$\frac{3}{4} \times \frac{3}{8} \times \frac{5}{16}$	$\frac{11}{16} \times \frac{7}{32}$	$\frac{3}{8} \times \frac{3}{8}$
$\frac{7}{16}$	$\frac{21}{32} \times \frac{3}{8}$	$\frac{7}{8} \times \frac{7}{32}$	$\frac{7}{8} \times \frac{7}{16} \times \frac{3}{8}$	$\frac{13}{16} \times \frac{1}{4}$	$\frac{7}{16} \times \frac{7}{16}$
$\frac{1}{2}$	$\frac{3}{4} \times \frac{7}{16}$	$1 \times \frac{1}{4}$	$1 \times \frac{1}{2} \times \frac{7}{16}$	$\frac{7}{8} \times \frac{1}{4}$	$\frac{1}{2} \times \frac{1}{2}$
$\frac{9}{16}$	$\frac{27}{32} \times \frac{1}{2}$	$1\frac{1}{8} \times \frac{9}{32}$	$1\frac{1}{8} \times \frac{9}{16} \times \frac{1}{2}$	$\frac{31}{32} \times \frac{9}{32}$	$\frac{9}{16} \times \frac{9}{16}$
$\frac{5}{8}$	$\frac{15}{16} \times \frac{17}{32}$	$1\frac{1}{4} \times \frac{5}{16}$	$1\frac{1}{4} \times \frac{5}{8} \times \frac{17}{32}$	$1\frac{1}{16} \times \frac{5}{16}$	$\frac{5}{8} \times \frac{5}{8}$
$\frac{3}{4}$	$1\frac{1}{8} \times \frac{5}{8}$	$1\frac{1}{2} \times \frac{3}{8}$	$1\frac{1}{2} \times \frac{3}{4} \times \frac{5}{8}$	$1\frac{1}{4} \times \frac{11}{32}$	$\frac{3}{4} \times \frac{3}{4}$
$\frac{7}{8}$	$1\frac{5}{16} \times \frac{3}{4}$	$1\frac{3}{4} \times \frac{7}{16}$	$1\frac{3}{4} \times \frac{7}{8} \times \frac{3}{4}$	$1\frac{7}{16} \times \frac{13}{32}$	$\frac{7}{8} \times \frac{7}{8}$
1	$1\frac{1}{2} \times \frac{7}{8}$	$2 \times \frac{1}{2}$	$2 \times 1 \times \frac{7}{8}$	$1\frac{5}{8} \times \frac{7}{16}$	1×1
$1\frac{1}{8}$	$1\frac{11}{16} \times 1$	$2\frac{1}{4} \times \frac{9}{16}$	$2\frac{1}{4} \times 1\frac{1}{8} \times 1$	. . .	
$1\frac{1}{4}$	$1\frac{7}{8} \times 1\frac{1}{8}$	$2\frac{1}{2} \times \frac{5}{8}$	$2\frac{1}{2} \times 1\frac{1}{4} \times 1\frac{1}{8}$	. . .	
$1\frac{3}{8}$	$2\frac{1}{16} \times 1\frac{1}{4}$	$2\frac{3}{4} \times \frac{11}{16}$	$2\frac{3}{4} \times 1\frac{3}{8} \times 1\frac{1}{4}$	. . .	
$1\frac{1}{2}$	$2\frac{1}{4} \times 1\frac{3}{8}$	$3 \times \frac{3}{4}$	$3 \times 1\frac{1}{2} \times 1\frac{3}{8}$	. . .	
$1\frac{5}{8}$	$2\frac{7}{16} \times 1\frac{1}{2}$	. . .	. . .	. . .	
$1\frac{3}{4}$	$2\frac{5}{8} \times 1\frac{5}{8}$				
$1\frac{7}{8}$	$2\frac{13}{16} \times 1\frac{3}{4}$	. . .	. . .		
2	$3 \times 1\frac{7}{8}$	. . .	. . .		

Heads of Lag Screws, Skein Screws and Tap Bolts will be made of same dimensions as given above for Square and Hexagon Head Bolts.

Square and Hexagon Bolt Heads made strictly to U. S. Standard proportions require extra upsets in order to obtain enough metal to form the heads, and consequently are much more expensive to make than bolt heads of the dimensions given above, which require but one upset, and are quite as strong and well proportioned as U. S. Standard heads.

Unless otherwise ordered we shall make all Countersunk Head Bolts at an angle of 35 degrees, excepting Boiler Patch Bolts, which will be made at an angle of 45 degrees.

Weight of Round Rolled Iron per Lineal Foot.

Dia.	Weight	Dia.	Weight	Dia.	Weight	Dia.	Weight	Dia.	Weight
1/16	.010	1 1/2	1.752	1 5/8	7.010	3 1/8	25.926	4 5/8	56.788
1/8	.041	5/8	2.032	1 3/4	8.128	3 1/4	28.040	4 3/4	59.900
3/16	.095	11/16	2.333	1 7/8	9.333	3 3/8	30.240	4 7/8	63.094
1/4	.165	1	2.654	2	10.616	3 1/2	32.512	5	66.752
5/16	.261	1 1/16	2.997	2 1/8	11.988	3 5/8	34.886	5 1/8	69.731
3/8	.373	1 1/8	3.360	2 1/4	13.440	3 3/4	37.332	5 1/4	73.172
7/16	.508	1 3/16	3.744	2 3/8	14.975	3 7/8	39.864	5 3/8	76.700
1/2	.663	1 1/4	4.172	2 1/2	16.688	4	42.464	5 1/2	80.304
9/16	.840	1 5/16	4.573	2 5/8	18.298	4 1/8	45.174	5 5/8	84.001
5/8	1.043	1 3/8	5.019	2 3/4	20.076	4 1/4	47.952	5 3/4	87.776
11/16	1.255	1 7/16	5.486	2 7/8	21.944	4 3/8	50.815	5 7/8	91.634
3/4	1.493	1 1/2	5.972	3	23.888	4 1/2	53.760	6	95.552

Weight of Square Rolled Iron per Lineal Foot.

Size	Weight	Size	Weight	Size	Weight	Size	Weight	Size	Weight
1/16	.013	13/16	2.231	2	13.520	3 3/8	38.503	4 3/4	76.264
1/8	.053	7/8	2.588	2 1/8	15.264	3 1/2	41.408	4 7/8	80.333
3/16	.119	15/16	2.971	2 1/4	17.112	3 5/8	44.418	5	84.480
1/4	.211	1	3.380	2 3/8	19.066	3 3/4	47.534	5 1/8	88.784
5/16	.330	1 1/16	3.816	2 1/2	21.120	3 7/8	50.756	5 1/4	93.168
3/8	.475	1 1/8	4.278	2 5/8	23.292	4	54.084	5 3/8	97.657
7/16	.647	1 1/4	5.280	2 3/4	25.560	4 1/8	57.517	5 1/2	102.240
1/2	.845	1 3/8	6.390	2 7/8	27.939	4 1/4	61.055	5 5/8	106.953
9/16	1.069	1 1/2	7.604	3	30.416	4 3/8	64.700	5 3/4	111.756
5/8	1.320	1 5/8	8.926	3 1/8	33.010	4 1/2	68.448	5 7/8	116.671
11/16	1.597	1 3/4	10.352	3 1/4	35.704	4 5/8	72.305	6	121.664
3/4	1.901	1 7/8	11.883	..	..	..	..	..	..

NOTE.—For cast iron deduct 1/8 part; for steel add 1/3; for copper add 1/7; for cast brass add 1/12; for lead add 1/2; for zinc deduct 1/13.

Weight of Flat Rolled Iron per Lineal Foot.

Width	THICKNESS									
	1/4	5/16	3/8	7/16	1/2	5/8	3/4	7/8	1	1 1/4
1/2	.422	.528	.634	.738	.845	. .	. .	. .	. .	. .
5/8	.528	.660	.792	.923	1.056	1.320	. .	. .	. .	. .
3/4	.633	.792	.950	1.108	1.265	1.584	1.901	. .	. .	. .
7/8	.738	.923	1.108	1.294	1.477	1.846	2.217	2.588	. .	. .
1	.845	1.056	1.267	1.478	1.690	2.112	2.534	2.956	3.380	. .
1 1/8	.950	1.187	1.425	1.663	1.901	2.375	2.850	3.326	3.802	4.752
1 1/4	1.056	1.320	1.584	1.848	2.112	2.640	3.168	3.696	4.224	5.280
1 3/8	1.161	1.452	1.742	2.032	2.325	2.904	3.484	4.065	4.646	5.808
1 1/2	1.266	1.584	1.900	2.217	2.535	3.168	3.802	4.435	5.069	6.337
1 5/8	1.372	1.716	2.059	2.402	2.746	3.432	4.119	4.805	5.492	6.864
1 3/4	1.479	1.848	2.218	2.589	2.957	3.696	4.435	5.178	5.914	7.393
1 7/8	1.584	1.980	2.376	2.772	3.168	3.960	4.752	5.544	6.336	7.921
2	1.689	2.112	2.534	2.957	3.379	4.224	5.069	5.914	6.758	8.448
2 1/8	1.795	2.244	2.693	3.141	3.591	4.488	5.386	6.283	7.181	8.977
2 1/4	1.900	2.376	2.851	3.326	3.802	4.752	5.703	6.653	7.604	9.505
2 3/8	2.006	2.508	3.009	3.511	4.013	5.016	6.019	7.022	8.025	10.032
2 1/2	2.112	2.640	3.168	3.696	4.224	5.280	6.336	7.392	8.448	10.560
2 3/4	2.323	2.904	3.485	4.066	4.647	5.808	6.970	8.132	9.294	11.617
3	2.535	3.168	3.802	4.435	5.069	6.337	7.604	8.871	10.138	12.673
3 1/4	2.746	3.432	4.119	4.805	5.492	6.865	8.237	9.610	10.983	13.730
3 1/2	2.957	3.696	4.436	5.175	5.914	7.393	8.871	10.350	11.828	14.785
3 3/4	3.168	3.960	4.752	5.544	6.336	7.921	9.505	11.089	12.673	15.841
4	3.380	4.224	5.069	5.914	6.759	8.448	10.138	11.828	13.518	16.897
4 1/2	3.802	4.752	5.703	6.653	7.604	9.504	11.406	13.306	15.208	19.010
5	4.224	5.280	6.336	7.392	8.449	10.560	12.673	14.784	16.897	21.122
5 1/2	4.647	5.808	6.970	8.132	9.294	11.616	13.940	16.264	18.587	23.234
6	5.070	6.337	7.604	8.871	10.138	12.674	15.208	17.742	20.276	25.346
7	5.914	7.392	8.872	10.350	11.828	14.786	17.742	20.700	23.656	29.570
8	6.760	8.448	10.138	11.828	13.518	16.896	20.276	23.656	27.036	33.794

Value of Iron per Gross Ton.

At from 1/10 to 4 9/10 cents per lb.

1/10c.	$2.24	1.1c.	$24.64	2.1c.	$47.04	3.1c.	$69.44	4.1c.	$91.84
2/10	4.48	1.2	26.88	2.2	49.28	3.2	71.68	4.2	94.08
3/10	6.72	1.3	29.12	2.3	51.52	3.3	73.92	4.3	96.32
4/10	8.96	1.4	31.36	2.4	53.76	3.4	76.16	4.4	98.56
5/10	11.20	1.5	33.60	2.5	56.00	3.5	78.40	4.5	100.80
6/10	13.44	1.6	35.84	2.6	58.24	3.6	80.64	4.6	103.04
7/10	15.68	1.7	38.08	2.7	60.48	3.7	82.88	4.7	105.28
8/10	17.92	1.8	40.32	2.8	62.72	3.8	85.12	4.8	107.52
9/10	20.16	1.9	42.56	2.9	64.96	3.9	87.36	4.9	109.76
1	22.40	2	44.80	3	67.20	4	89.60	. .	. .

FORGINGS.

We manufacture largely

Arch Bars and Body Bolsters,

and drill the holes in a multiple press, thus insuring accuracy and uniformity at the lowest cost.

ALSO ALL KINDS OF

Car Forgings, Anchor Bolts, Stirrups,

Brake Levers, Link Pins,

Punched and Bent Plates, Tie Rods for Cable

and Electric Roads,

Forgings for Electric Railways, Arm Braces

for Telegraph Poles, Bridle Irons,

and all the various forgings used in structural work. Our facilities enable us to give prompt attention to this class of work at reasonable prices.

Cuts of some ordinary forgings are illustrated in the pages following.

Estimates furnished on application.

Forgings for Car Work.

Fig. 72.

Standard Arch Bar.

Fig. 73.

Retaining Lip Arch Bar.

Forgings for Car Work.

Fig. 74.

Brake Lever.

Fig. 75.

Brake Lever Connecting Rod.

Fig. 76.

Brake Hanger Carrier.

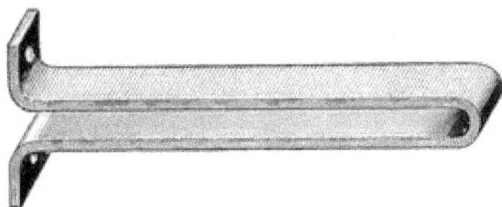

Fig. 77.

Brake Lever Guide.

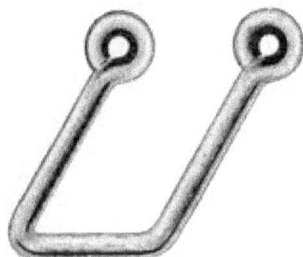

Fig 78.

Brake Hanger.

Car Forgings.

Fig. 79.

Dead Lever Guide.

Fig. 80.

Brake Beam Safety Hanger Carrier.

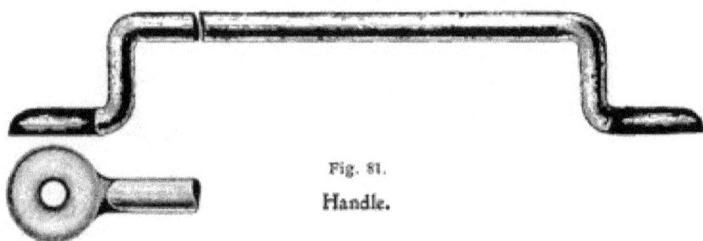

Fig. 81.

Handle.

Fig. 82.

Step.

Forgings for Structural Work.

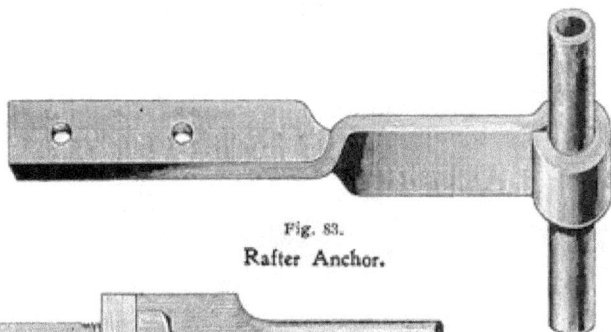

Fig. 83.
Rafter Anchor.

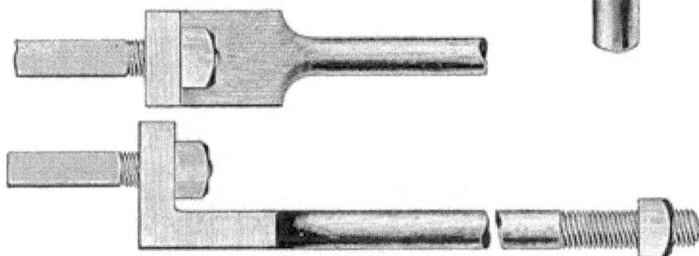

Fig. 84.
Expansion Bolts with Tie Rivets.

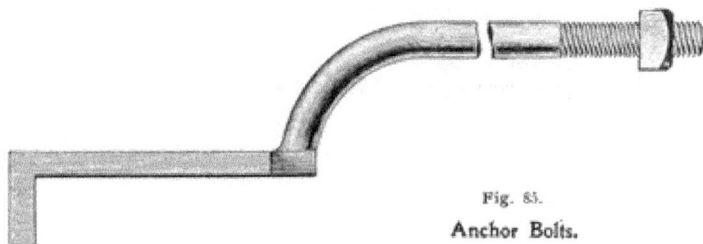

Fig. 85.
Anchor Bolts.

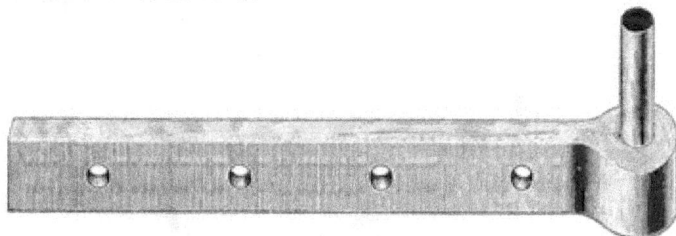

Fig. 86.
Hinges.

Forgings for Structural Work.

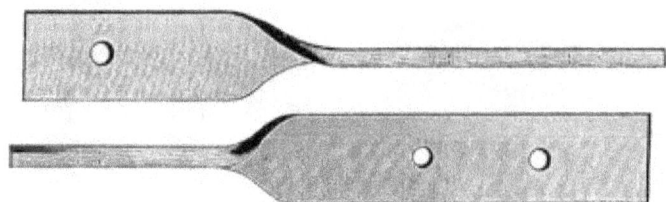

Fig. 87
Twisted Strap.

Fig 88.
Strap Bolt.

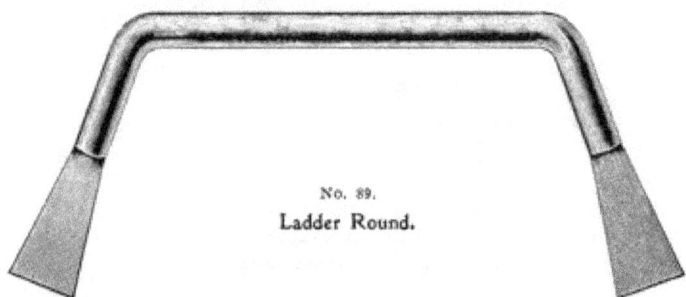

No. 89.
Ladder Round.

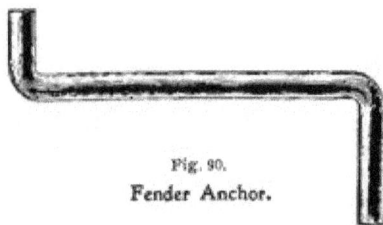

Fig. 90.
Fender Anchor.

Forgings for Electric Railway Construction.

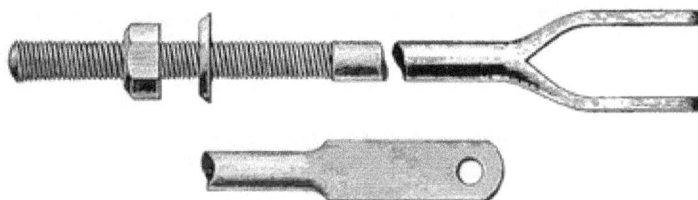

Fig. 91.

Trolley Span Wire Fork Bolt.

Fig. 92.

Bracket Rod.

Fig. 93.

Skew Rod—Double Eyes.

Fig. 94.

Pole Strap.

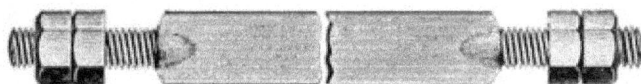

Fig. 95.

Tie Rod.

Forgings for Automatic Couplers.

Fig. 96.

Back Link Pin.

Fig. 97.

Knuckle Pin.

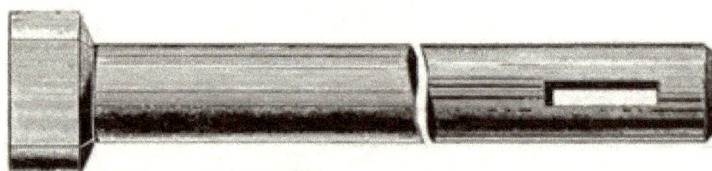

Fig. 98.

Draw Head Bolt.

Fig 99.

Draw Head Bolt with Nut.

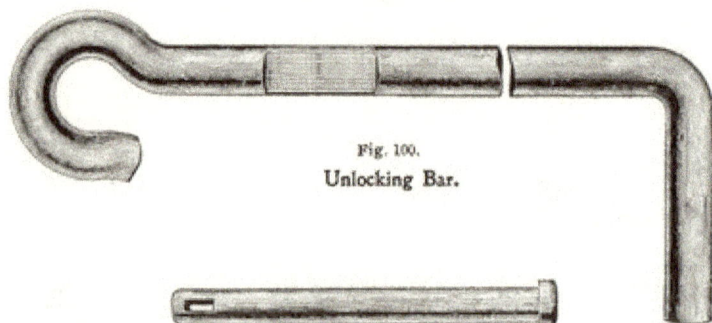

Fig. 100.

Unlocking Bar.

Fig. 101.

Pivot Pin.

Rods, Stirrups, etc., for Structural Work.

Fig. 102.

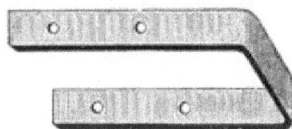
Fig. 103.

Fig. 104.

Fig. 105.

Fig. 106.

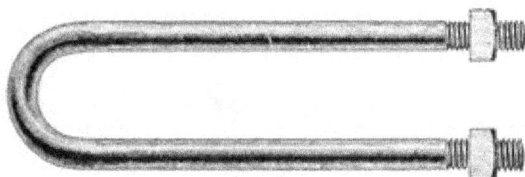
Fig 107.

Special Bolts.

Fig. 108.
Welded Eye Bolt.

Fig. 109.
Tee Head Bolt.

Fig. 110.
Collar Bolt.

Fig. 111.
Ore-Washery Screw.

Fig. 112.
Deck Bolt, Pan Head,
Square Neck.

Fig. 113.
Joint Bolt, Oblong Nut, Cone Point.

Fig. 114.
Square Head, Square Neck,
Machine Bolt.

Fig. 115.
Screen Bolt, Cube Head.

Fig. 116.
Style of Slotted Head.

Fig. 117.
Eye Lag Screw.

Fig. 118.
Lag Screw Hook.

TELEGRAPHIC CODE INDEX.

TELEGRAPHIC CODE.

CORRESPONDENCE.

Answer by mail . . . . Abandon.
Answer by telegraph . . . . Abase.
Referring to our letter of . . . . Abatis.
Referring to your letter of . . . . Abbess.
See our letter of to-day, giving full particulars . . . . Abdicate.
Have received no reply to ours of . . . . Abdomen.
Referring to your telegram of . . . . Abet.
Referring to our telegram of . . . . Abhor.
Wire reply to ours of . . . . Abide.
Letter referred to not received. Send copy . . . . Abject.
Letter referred to not received. Wire substance . . . . Ablaze.
Letter received. Will have our prompt attention . . . . Aboard.

PRICE—Inquiries.

Quote best price and terms by wire, F. O. B. mill . . . . Academy.
Quote best price and terms by wire, delivered here . . . . Achieve.
Quote best price and terms by mail, F. O. B. mill . . . . Acme.
Quote best price and terms by mail, delivered here . . . . Acorn.
Can you make quick shipment, { F. O. B. mill . . . . Acoustic.
     and at what price?   { delivered here . . . . Acquaint.

PRICE—Answers.

Specifications insufficient. Give full particulars . . . . Acquire.
Not in position to quote on your inquiry of . . . . Acrid.
We name you on your inquiry of . . . . Acrobat.
We name you for prompt acceptance . . . . Across.
We name you for immediate shipment . . . . Acting.
We name you for shipment in . . . . Action.
We quote you for spot cash . . . . Actual.
We quote you for sight draft with B | L . . . . Acumen.
We quote you for 30 days net . . . . Acute.
We quote you for 60 days net . . . . Adage.
We quote you for 60 days, 2 per cent. cash 10 days . . . . Adamant.
We quote you for 90 days net . . . . Adder.
We quote you for usual terms . . . . Addict.
Cannot amend our quotation . . . . Adept.
Cannot accept order at price named . . . . Adhere.
We will accept your offer . . . . Adipose.

STOCK—Inquiries.

How soon can you ship us . . . . Admire.
Have you in stock . . . . Admission
How soon could you make and ship . . . . Admit.
How soon could you begin and complete shipment . . . . Admonish

TELEGRAPHIC CODE.

STOCK—Replies.

Can ship all from stock . . . . Adobe.
Can ship an assortment at once, balance in . . . . Adoption.
Can ship complete in . . . . Adorn.
Can ship within a week from receipt of order . . . . Adrift.
Can make shipment within time named . . . . Adulation.
Cannot make within time named . . . . Adult.
Cannot furnish the goods, your inquiry of . . . . Advent.

ORDERS—Instructions.

Ship what you can at once . . . . Adverb.
Ship if you can ship to-day . . . . Adviser.
Ship by express . . . . Advocate.
Ship by freight . . . . Affable.
Ship by boat . . . . Affair.
Enter order as per our inquiry of . . . . Aggress.
Enter order at your quotation of . . . . Aghast.
Enter order if you can ship within a week . . . . Agile.
Enter order if you can ship immediately . . . . Agility.
Hold for instructions our order of . . . . Affect.
Suspend work on our order of . . . . Affection.
Cancel our order of . . . . Affiance.
Add to our order of . . . . Affiliate.
Duplicate our order of . . . . Affinity.
Hurry shipment our order of . . . . Affirm.
When will you ship our order of . . . . Affix.
Trace our shipment of . . . . Afflict.

ORDERS—Replies.

Have entered order as per yours of . . . . Affright.
Cannot ship within time named your order of . . . . Afloat.
We have shipped to-day by freight . . . . Afresh.
We have shipped to-day by express . . . . Agape.
We have shipped to-day by boat . . . . Agnate.
Now working on your order. Will ship on . . . . Agonize.
Goods all made. Cannot cancel . . . . Agrarian.
Goods referred to were shipped on . . . . Agreed.
Awaiting your specifications . . . . Aground.
Mail shipping directions. Your order of . . . . Ailment.
Wire shipping directions. Your order of . . . . Album.
Will hold your order, awaiting letter . . . . Albumen.

TELEGRAPHIC CODE.

BOLTS—Kinds.

		Square Nuts	Hexagon Nuts	Thumb Nuts
Machine Bolts with	Square Heads	Babette	Baluster	Behoof
	Hexagon Heads . . .	Baboon	Bamboo	Belabor
	Button Heads	Babylon	Bangle	Belated
Carriage Bolts with	Squeezed Necks . . .	Bachelor	Banish	Belay
	Full Square Necks . .	Backbone	Bankrupt	Beldam
	Skew Head	Backward	Banner	Belfry
	Countersunk Heads .	Bacon	Banneret	Belgic
Bolt Ends		Badger	Bannock	Belial
Rods or Double Bolt Ends		Baffle	Banquet	
Sleigh Shoe Bolts		Bailiff	Bantam	
Tire Bolts		Bairn		
Stove Bolts	Flat Heads	Balcony		
	Round Heads	Ballast		
Stove Rods		Balloon		

	Button Heads	Square Heads	Hexagon Heads
Machine Bolt Blanks	Balsam	Barbery	Belike
Key Bolts	Baltic	Barbican	Bellman
Lag Screws, common point		Barebone	Bellicose
Coach Screws, gimlet point		Beadle	Bellow
Skein Bolts		Beauty	Bemoan
Set Screws, forged		Beaver	Benedict
Tap Bolts, forged		Becalm	Benefice

		Right Hand	Left Hand
Plow Bolts	Square Countersunk Heads	Bedding	Benison
	Round Countersunk Heads	Beetle	Benumb
	Key Heads	Beggar	Bergamot
	Reverse Key Heads	Beginner	Bestow
	Round Head, Square Neck	Behemoth	Betide

TELEGRAPHIC CODE.

RIVETS, DRIFT BOLTS, TRACK BOLTS.

	Boiler	Bridge	Norway	Steel
Rivets — Cone Heads	Blabber	Blackness	Bleeding	Bombastic
Button Heads	Blackball	Bladder	Blemish	Bonbon
Wagon Box Heads	Blackbird	Blamable	Blessed	Bondage
Flat Heads	Blackfish	Blameless	Blighted	Bondmaid
Countersunk Heads	Blackleg	Blanched	Blindfold	Boneset

		Chisel Points	Blunt Points	No Points
Square Drift Bolts	Button Heads	Blandness	Blindness	Bonfire
	Ctsk. "	Blanket	Blinkard	Bonnet
	No "	Blarney	Blissful	Booby
Round Drift Bolts	Button "	Blasting	Blister	Bookcase
	Ctsk. "	Bleacher	Bloated	Bookstore
	No "	Bleakly	Blockade	Bookworm

		$1\frac{3}{4} \times \frac{3}{4}$ Nut	$1\frac{1}{2} \times \frac{3}{4}$ Nut
Track Bolts, Square Nuts.	$\frac{3}{4} \times 3$	Blockhead	Bopeep
	$3\frac{1}{4}$	Blonde	Borax
	$3\frac{1}{2}$	Bloodshed	Border
	$3\frac{3}{4}$	Blooming	Boreas
	4	Blossom	Borrow
	$4\frac{1}{2}$	Blotter	Botanic
Track Bolts, Hex. Nuts.	$\frac{3}{4} \times 3$	Blowpipe	Bottle
	$3\frac{1}{4}$	Blubber	Bottomless
	$3\frac{1}{2}$	Bludgeon	Boundary
	$3\frac{3}{4}$	Bluntness	Bounteous
	4	Bluster	Bounty
	$4\frac{1}{2}$	Boarder	Bouquet

	Square Nuts	Hexagon Nuts
Track Bolts, $\frac{5}{8} \times 2\frac{1}{2}$	Boaster	Bovine
$2\frac{3}{4}$	Boathook	Bowery
3	Boatman	Bowline
$3\frac{1}{4}$	Boatswain	Bowsprit
$3\frac{1}{2}$	Bobbin	Boxer
$\frac{9}{16} \times 2\frac{1}{2}$	Bobtail	Boyhood
$2\frac{3}{4}$	Bobwig	Bracelet
3	Bodice	Bracket
$3\frac{1}{2}$	Bodkin	Braggart
$\frac{1}{2} \times 1\frac{1}{2}$	Boggle	Brahma
$1\frac{3}{4}$	Bohea	Brakeman
2	Boldness	Brandied
$2\frac{1}{4}$	Bolster	Bravado
$2\frac{1}{2}$	Bolus	Bravery
$2\frac{3}{4}$	Bombard	Brazen

TELEGRAPHIC CODE.

PLAIN COLD PRESSED NUTS.

	Manufacturers' Standard	Narrow Gauge	U. S. Standard
$\frac{7}{16}$ Square	Cabbage	Capable	
$\frac{1}{2}$	Cabinet	Caparison	Carcass
$\frac{9}{16}$	Cable	Capillary	Carded
$\frac{5}{8}$	Caboose	Capital	Cardinal
$\frac{11}{16}$	Cackling	Capped	Career
$\frac{3}{4}$	Cadence	Capricious	Caressed
$\frac{13}{16}$	Caitiff	. . . . .	Caricature
$\frac{7}{8}$	Cajole	Capricorn	Carman
$\frac{15}{16}$	Calabash	Capsize	Carnage
$\frac{7}{8}$	Calamity	Capstan	Carnation
1	Calamus	Capsule	Carolina
$1\frac{1}{8}$	Calcined	Captive	Carousal
$1\frac{1}{4}$	Calculator	Captor	Carpenter
$1\frac{3}{8}$	Caldron	. . . . .	Carpet
$1\frac{1}{2}$	Calendar	. . . . .	Carping
$1\frac{5}{8}$	Calico	. . . . .	Cartoon
$1\frac{3}{4}$	Calker	. . . . .	Cartwright
$1\frac{7}{8}$	Callous	. . . . .	Cascade
2	Calmness	. . . . .	Casement
$2\frac{1}{8}$	Calomel	. . . . .	Cassock
$2\frac{1}{4}$	Caloric	. . . . .	Castanet
$\frac{1}{2}$ Hexagon	Calumet	. . . . .	Castle
$\frac{9}{16}$	Calumny	. . . . .	Catamount
$\frac{5}{8}$	Calvin	. . . . .	Catacomb
$\frac{11}{16}$	Cambrics	. . . . .	Cataract
$\frac{1}{2}$	Camomile	Captured	Catcher
$\frac{13}{16}$	Campaign	. . . . .	Catchup
$\frac{5}{8}$	Camphor	Caravans	Catechise
$\frac{3}{4}$	Canal	Caraway	Category
$\frac{7}{8}$	Canary	Carbine	Caterer
1	Candid	Carbuncle	Catfish
$1\frac{1}{8}$	Canebrake	. . . . .	Cathartic
$1\frac{1}{4}$	Canister	. . . . .	Cathedral
$1\frac{3}{8}$	Cannibal	. . . . .	Catmint
$1\frac{1}{2}$	Cannon	. . . . .	Caucus
$1\frac{5}{8}$	Canopy	. . . . .	Caudal
$1\frac{3}{4}$	Cantata	. . . . .	Causeway
$1\frac{7}{8}$	Canteen	. . . . .	Caustic
2	Canticle	. . . . .	Cavalcade
$2\frac{1}{8}$	Canvas	. . . . .	Cavalier
$2\frac{1}{4}$	Capapie	. . . . .	Cavern

TELEGRAPHIC CODE.

COLD PRESSED, CHAMFERED, TRIMMED AND REAMED.
U. S. STANDARD SIZES.

	Square	Hexagon		Square	Hexagon
$\frac{1}{16}$	Fable	Falsify	$1\frac{1}{8}$	Fainting	Farcical
$\frac{1}{8}$	Fabricate	Falter	$1\frac{1}{4}$	Fairness	Farewell
$\frac{3}{16}$	Fabulous	Familiar	$1\frac{3}{8}$	Faithful	Farinaceous
$\frac{1}{4}$	Facetious	Famine	$1\frac{1}{2}$	Falchion	Farmer
$\frac{5}{16}$	Facility	Famished	$1\frac{5}{8}$	Falconry	Farrago
$\frac{3}{8}$	Facsimile	Fanatic	$1\frac{3}{4}$	Fallacy	Farthing
$\frac{7}{16}$	Faction	Fanciful	$1\frac{7}{8}$	Fallible	Fascinate
$\frac{1}{2}$	Factorage	Fangled	2	Fallow	Fashion
$\frac{3}{4}$	Faculty	Fantastic	$2\frac{1}{8}$	False	Fastidious
$\frac{7}{8}$	Fagot	Fantasy	$2\frac{1}{4}$	Falsetto	Fatalism
1	Failure	Farfamed			

WASHERS.

		Wrought, Round	Cast	Plate, Square
$\frac{3}{16}$	Riveting	Fealty		
$\frac{1}{16}$	Washer	Fearless		
$\frac{1}{4}$	Riveting	Feasible		
$\frac{1}{4}$	Washer	Feather		
$\frac{5}{16}$	. . . .	Feature		
$\frac{3}{8}$	. . . .	Febrile		
$\frac{7}{16}$	. . . .	Fecula		
$\frac{1}{2}$	. . . .	Federal	Festal	Fidget
$\frac{9}{16}$	. . . .	Feeble	Festoon	Figment
$\frac{5}{8}$	. . . .	Felicitate	Fetlock	Filbert
$\frac{3}{4}$	. . . .	Feline	Feudal	Filiform
$\frac{7}{8}$	. . . .	Fellow	Feverfew	Fillet
1	. . . .	Felucca	Fibrous	Filmy
$1\frac{1}{8}$	. . . .	Fennel	Fickle	Filtrate
$1\frac{1}{4}$	. . . .	Ferment	Fiction	Finale
$1\frac{3}{8}$	. . . .	Ferocious	Fictitious	Finery
$1\frac{1}{2}$	. . . .	Ferrule	Fiddle	Finger
$1\frac{5}{8}$	. . . .	Ferry		
$1\frac{3}{4}$	. . . .	Fertile		
$1\frac{7}{8}$	. . . .	Fervent		
2	. . . .	Fervor		

TELEGRAPHIC CODE.

HOT PRESSED NUTS.

	Manufacturers' Standard	Narrow Gauge	U. S. Standard
7/16 Square	Gabbler	Generation	
1/2	Gadding	Genet	Gibbet
9/16	Gadfly	Genial	Giddy
5/8	Gaffer	Genitive	Gigantic
11/16	Gainsay	Genteel	Giggler
3/4	Gaiter	Gentian	Gilse
13/16	Galaxy	. . . . .	Gimcrack
7/8	Galiot	Gentile	Ginger
15/16	Gallant	Geography	Gingham
	Galleon	Geology	Gipsy
1	Gallican	Geometry	Girdle
1 1/8	Gallop	Geranium	Gizzard
1 1/4	Gallows	German	Glacier
1 3/8	Galvanic	. . . . .	Gladiator
1 1/2	Galvanism	. . . . .	Gladsome
1 5/8	Gambler	. . . . .	Gladwin
1 3/4	Gamboge	. . . . .	Glanders
1 7/8	Gambrel	. . . . .	Glaring
2	Gamester	. . . . .	Glassy
2 1/8	Gammon	. . . . .	Gleeful
2 1/4	Gamut	. . . . .	Glibness
2 3/8	Gander	. . . . .	Glimmer
2 1/2	Gangrene	. . . . .	Glisten
2 3/4	Gangway	. . . . .	Globule
3	Gantlet	. . . . .	Gloomy
1/2 Hexagon	Garbage	. . . . .	Glorious
9/16	Garden	. . . . .	Glowing
5/8	Garland	. . . . .	Glutton
11/16	Garment	. . . . .	Gnarled
3/4	Garnish	Germinate	Goldfinch
13/16	Garret	. . . . .	Goldleaf
7/8	Garrison	Gesture	Gondola
15/16	Garter	Gewgaw	Gormand
	Gasconade	Ghastly	Gosling
1	Gasket	Giant	Gossamer
1 1/8	Gaslight	. . . . .	Gotham
1 1/4	Gastric	. . . . .	Governess
1 3/8	Gateway	. . . . .	Gowan
1 1/2	Gathering	. . . . .	Gradient
1 5/8	Gaudy	. . . . .	Grammar
1 3/4	Gauger	. . . . .	Granary
1 7/8	Gawky	. . . . .	Grandam
2	Gazette	. . . . .	Grandson
2 1/8	Gazetteer	. . . . .	Granger
2 1/4	Geared	. . . . .	Granite
2 3/8	Gelatin	. . . . .	Granular
2 1/2	Gelding	. . . . .	Grapnel
2 5/8	Gemini	. . . . .	Gratitude
3	Gender	. . . . .	Gravel

TELEGRAPHIC CODE.

QUANTITY.

	Only	Standard Size Package	Hundreds	Thousands	Carloads
⅛	. . . . .	. . . . .	Malaria	Modernize	
¼	. . . . .	Manful	Mammal	Matchless	Morass
1	Macaroni	Manganese	Mandarin	Mattock	Morbid
2	Maccoboy	Mangled	Masticate	Mediator	Morbose
3	Mackerel	Mango	Mastif	Memory	Mordant
4	Madam	Mangrove	Mastodon	Mendicant	Moribund
5	Madcap	Manhood	Matchless	Mention	Mormon
6	Madder	Maniac	Maternal	Merchant	Morpheus
7	Madeira	Manifest	Matins	Merciless	Morsel
8	Madhouse	Manikin	Matrice	Mercury	Mortar
9	Madman	Manna	Matrimony	Meridian	Mortise
10	Madrigal	Mansion	Mattock	Merriment	Mosaic
11	Magazine	Manual	Mature	Modesty	
12	Magic	Manumit	Maxim	Modify	
13	Magician	Manuscript	Mayday	Modulate	
14	Magistrate	Maple	Mayflower	Mohair	
15	Magnesia	Marauder	Maypole	Metallic	
16	Magnet	Marble	Mazarine	Mohawk	
17	Magnolia	Marching	Maze	Molasses	
18	Mahogany	Marginal	Mechanic	Molecule	
19	Maiden	Marigold	Medallion	Momentum	
20	Mainland	Mariner	Mediator	Monarchy	
21	Maintain	Marjoram	Medical	Mongrel	
22	Majesty	Market	Medicine	Monition	
23	Major	Marksman	Meditation	Monitor	
⋅24	Malady	Marmot	Melancholy	Monkery	
25	Malaria	Maroon	Melody	Monkhood	
26	Malcontent	Marplot	Member	Monody	
27	Malignant	Marquis	Membrane	Monogram	
28	Mallard	Marrow	Memento	Monolith	
29	Mallet	Marshal	Memorial	Monome	
30	Mallow	Marten	Memory	Monopoly	
40	Maltster	Martyr	Mendicant	Monotone	
50	Mammal	Marvel	Mention	Monsoon	
60	Mammoth	Masculine	Merchant	Monster	
70	Manacle	Mashed	Merciless	Montero	
80	Manager	Masking	Mercury	Monument	
90	Mandamus	Mason	Meridian	Moonbeam	
100	Mandarin	Masquerade	Merriment	Moonshine	
125	Mandate	Massacre	Messenger	Moorish	
150	Mandible	Massive	Metallic	Moppet	
175	Mandrake	Mastery	Moderate	Moralize	

TELEGRAPHIC CODE.

DISCOUNTS.

Per Cent.		Per Cent.		Per Cent.	
2	Dabble	50	Dawn	75 & 5	Despotism
2½	Dagger	50 & 2½	Daybreak	75 & 7½	Dessert
3	Dainty	50 & 5	Daylight	75 & 10	Destiny
5	Dairy	50 & 7½	Daysman	75 & 12½	Destitute
7½	Dally	55	Deacon	75 & 15	Destruction
10	Dalliance	55 & 2½	Deanery	75 & 17½	Desuetude
12½	Damaged	55 & 5	Decade	80	Desultory
15	Damascus	55 & 7½	Decadence	80 & 2½	Detach
17½	Damask	55 & 10	Decamped	80 & 5	Detail
20	Damper	60	Decimal	80 & 7½	Detective
20 & 2½	Damsel	60 & 2½	Declaimer	80 & 10	Deterge
20 & 5	Damson	60 & 5	Decoction	80 & 12½	Determent
25	Dancer	60 & 7½	Defiance	80 & 15	Detersion
25 & 2½	Dandelion	60 & 10	Delicate	80 & 17½	Detest
25 & 5	Dandruf	65	Delineate	80 & 20	Dethrone
30	Danewort	65 & 2½	Demagogue	80, 20 & 2½	Detonate
30 & 2½	Danger	65 & 5	Demijohn	85	Detriment
30 & 5	Dapper	65 & 7½	Demonstrate	85 & 2½	Devastate
35	Daring	65 & 10	Demurrage	85 & 5	Develop
35 & 2½	Darkness	70	Denizen	85 & 7½	Deviate
35 & 5	Darling	70 & 2½	Dentist	85 & 10	Devisable
40	Darnel	70 & 5	Dependence	85 & 12½	Devolve
40 & 2½	Dashing	70 & 7½	Deplorable	85 & 15	Devoted
40 & 5	Dative	70 & 10	Deportment	85 & 17½	Devourer
45	Dauber	70 & 12½	Deposition	85 & 20	Devoutly
45 & 2½	Daughter	70 & 15	Derogate	85, 20 & 2½	Dewdrop
45 & 5	Dauntless	75	Desolate	85 & 25	Dextral
45 & 7½	Dauphin	75 & 2½	Desperado		

TELEGRAPHIC CODE.

PRICES PER HUNDRED POUNDS.

$		$		$	
1.50	Pacific	2.50	Parabolic	3.50	Pastry
2½	Packet	2½	Parachute	5	Pasture
5	Packhorse	5	Paradise	3.60	Patchwork
7½	Paddle	7½	Paradox	5	Patentee
1.60	Paddock	2.60	Paragon	3.70	Pathway
2½	Pagan	2½	Paragraph	5	Patience
5	Pageant	5	Parallax	3.80	Patriarch
7½	Pagoda	7½	Parapet	5	Patrician
1.70	Painless	2.70	Paraphrase	3.90	Patriot
2½	Painter	2½	Parasite	5	Patrol
5	Palace	5	Parasol	4.00	Patronage
7½	Palanquin	7½	Parboiled	5	Pattern
1.80	Palate	2.80	Parcel	4.10	Pauper
2½	Palatine	2½	Parchment	5	Pavillion
5	Palisade	5	Pardon	4.20	Payday
7½	Palladium	7½	Paregoric	5	Paymaster
1.90	Pallitte	2.90	Parentage	4.30	Pedagogue
2½	Palmetto	2½	Parish	5	Pedantic
5	Palmistry	5	Parishioner	4.40	Peddler
7½	Palpable	7½	Parley	5	Pedestal
2.00	Palpitate	3.00	Parliament	4.50	Pedigree
2½	Palsied	2½	Parochial	5	Peerage
5	Pamper	5	Parody	4.60	Peerless
7½	Pamphlet	7½	Parrot	5	Pelican
2.10	Panacea	3.10	Parsley	4.70	Pellmell
2½	Pancake	2½	Partaken	5	Pemmican
5	Pandore	5	Partial	4.80	Penance
7½	Panel	7½	Participant	5	Penchant
2.20	Pangalin	3.20	Particle	4.90	Pendulum
2½	Panicle	2½	Partisan	5	Penetrate
5	Pannier	5	Partition	5.00	Penguin
7½	Panorama	7½	Partner	5	Peninsula
2.30	Pantheist	3.30	Partridge	5.10	Penitence
2½	Pantheon	2½	Passage	5	Penknife
5	Pantograph	5	Passenger	5.20	Penman
7½	Pantomime	7½	Passion	5	Pennate
2.40	Pantry	3.40	Passive	5.30	Pension
2½	Papacy	2½	Pasteboard	5	Penstock
5	Pappoose	5	Pastime	5.40	Pentagon
7½	Papyrus	7½	Pastoral	5	Pepper

TELEGRAPHIC CODE.

Sizes of Bolts, Rivets 3-16 to 1-2 Diameter, up to 12 inches Long.

	$\frac{3}{16}$	$\frac{1}{4}$	$\frac{5}{16}$	$\frac{3}{8}$	$\frac{7}{16}$	$\frac{1}{2}$
½	Saber	Sally	Sanguinary	Saturant	Scamper	
⅝	Sable	Sallyport	Sanguine	Saturate	Scandal	
¾	Sabulous	Salmon	Sanhedrim	Saturn	Scandalize	
⅞	Saccharine	Saloon	Sanitary	Saturnian	Scandalous	Schooling
1	Saccharoid	Salsify	Sanity	Satyr	Scandent	Schooner
1⅛	Sachem	Saltant	Sanscrit	Saucebox	Scanned	Sciatic
1¼	Sackage	Saltern	Sapid	Saucer	Scanning	Science
1⅜	Sackbut	Saltish	Sapidness	Saucily	Scantily	Scientific
1½	Sackcloth	Saltness	Sapient	Sauciness	Scantling	Scintillant
1⅝	Sacked	Saltpan	Sapless	Saunter	Scantiness	Scioptic
1¾	Sacrifice	Saltpit	Sapling	Saurian	Scantly	Sclavonic
1⅞	Sacridge	Saltpeter	Sapped	Sausage	Scape	Scoff
2	Sacristan	Salubrious	Sapphie	Savable	Scapegoat	Scoffer
2¼	Sadden	Salutary	Sapphire	Savage	Scapegrace	Scold
2½	Saddle	Salutation	Sappiness	Savagely	Scapeless	Scolding
2¾	Saddling	Salute	Saraband	Savageness	Scapement	Scoop
3	Sadiron	Salvable	Saracen	Savant	Scapula	Scooped
3¼	Sadness	Salvage	Sarcasm	Saved	Scapulary	Scoopnet
3½	Safeguard	Salvation	Sarcastic	Savor	Scarabee	Scorch
3¾	Safeness	Salver	Sarcenet	Savorless	Scarcely	Scorched
4	Saffron	Samaritan	Sarcode	Savory	Scarecrow	Scoria
4¼	Sagacious	Sambo	Sarcoline	Sawney	Scarf	Scoriform
4½	Sagacity	Sameness	Sardine	Sawpit	Scarfing	Scorner
4¾	Sagely	Samp	Sardonian	Sawset	Scarify	Scornful
5	Sago	Samphire	Sardonyx	Sawyer	Scarlatina	Scorpion
5¼	Sailing	Sampler	Sarsaparilla	Saxifrage	Scarlet	Scotch
5½	Sailloft	Sanable	Sassafas	Saxon	Scathful	Scottish
5¾	Sailor	Sanation	Sash	Saxonism	Scatter	Scoundrel
6	Sailyard	Sanative	Satan	Scabbard	Scattering	Scourged
6¼	Sainted	Sanctify	Satanic	Scabrous	Scavenger	Scow
6½	Saintlike	Sanction	Satanical	Scaffold	Scenery	Scowl
6¾	Salable	Sanctuary	Satanism	Scaffolding	Scenic	Scowled
7	Salad	Sanctum	Satchel	Scalade	Scentful	Scrabble
7¼	Salam	Sand	Satellite	Scald	Scepter	Scrag
7½	Salary	Sandal	Satiate	Scaleless	Scepticism	Scraggy
7¾	Saleratus	Sandbag	Satiation	Scalene	Schedule	Scragginess
8	Salework	Sandbath	Satiety	Scaliness	Schematist	Scramble
8½	Salic	Sandbox	Satinet	Scallion	Scheme	Scraper
9	Salicine	Sanded	Satire	Scallop	Schemer	Scratch
9½	Salient	Sandpaper	Satirical	Scalp	Scholar	Scratching
10	Salify	Sandstone	Satirist	Scalped	Scholarly	Scrawled
10½	Saline	Sandwich	Satisfaction	Scaly	Scholarship	Scrawny
11	Saliva	Saneness	Satisfied	Scamble	Scholastic	Scream
11½	Salivate	Sangaree	Satisfy	Scambler	Scholium	Screamer
12	Sallow	Sangfroid	Satrap	Scamp	School	Screech

TELEGRAPHIC CODE.

Sizes of Bolts, Rivets 9-16 to 1 1-8 Diameter, up to 15 Inches Long.

$\frac{9}{16}$	$\frac{5}{8}$	$\frac{3}{4}$	$\frac{7}{8}$	1	$1\frac{1}{8}$
1 Screechowl					
1¼ Screened	Seamark	Sedan			
1½ Scribbler	Seamless	Sedate	Semicircle		
1¾ Scribner	Seamster	Sedately	Semicolon	Separator	
2 Scripture	Seamy	Sedateness	Seminal	Sepawn	Serrate
2¼ Scrivener	Seanymph	Sedative	Seminary	Sepoy	
2½ Scrofula	Seaport	Sedentary	Seminate	Septenary	Serrated
2¾ Scroll	Search	Sedgy	Seminateor	Septennial	
3 Scrotiform	Searcher	Sediment	Semitone	Septuagint	Serum
3¼ Scrub	Searching	Sedition	Semitonic	Septum	
3½ Scrubby	Searcloth	Seductive	Senary	Septuple	Serval
3¾ Scruple	Searisk	Sedulity	Senate	Sepulchre	
4 Scrupulous	Searoom	Sedulous	Senator	Sepulture	Servant
4¼ Scrutineer	Seashell	Seedling	Senatorial	Sequacious	
4½ Scrutiny	Seaside	Seedtime	Seneschal	Sequel	Served
4¾ Scuddle	Season	Seedy	Senile	Sequence	
5 Scuffle	Seasoning	Seeking	Senior	Sequester	Service
5¼ Scullery	Seaterm	Seeker			
5½ Scullion	Seaward	Seem	Seniority	Sequin	Serving
5¾ Sculptor	Seawater	Seeming			
6 Scummer	Seawolf	Seemliness	Senna	Seraglio	Servitor
6¼ Scupper	Sebaceous	Seemly			
6½ Scurfiness	Secant	Seesaw	Sennight	Seraph	Servitude
6¾ Scurrile	Seceder	Seethe			
7 Scurrilous	Secession	Segment	Sensate	Seraphic	Sesame
7¼ Scurvily	Seclude	Segregate			
7½ Scurviness	Seclusion	Segregation	Sensation	Seraphim	Sesamum
7¾ Scurvy	Secondary	Selah			
8 Scutate	Secondly	Seldom	Senseless	Serenade	Sessile
8½ Scutcheon	Secrecy	Select	Sensible	Serene	Session
9 Scutiform	Secret	Selection	Sensific	Serenely	Sesspool
9½ Scuttle	Secretary	Selectmen	Sensitive	Serfdom	Sesterce
10 Scythe	Secretion	Selector	Sensorial	Serge	Setaceous
10½ Scythian	Sectarian	Self	Sensorium	Sergeant	Seton
11 Seaboard	Sectarist	Selfish	Sentence	Serial	Setter
11½ Seaborn	Sectile	Selfishly	Sentenced	Series	Settlement
12 Seabreeze	Section	Selfishness	Sentential	Seriously	Setto
12½ Seacoast	Sectional	Selfsame	Sentiment	Sermon	Sever
13 Seafarer	Sector	Selvedge	Sentimental	Sermonize	Severance
13½ Seafowl	Secular	Semaphore	Sentinel	Seroon	Severity
14 Seagirt	Secularize	Semblance	Sentry	Serosity	Sewed
14½ Seagrass	Secured	Semester	Sepal	Serpent	Sewerage
15 Seaman	Security	Semibreve	Separation	Serpentine	Sextant

TELEGRAPHIC CODE.

Sizes of Bolts, 1-4 to 9-16 Inclusive, Longer than 12 Inches.

	1/4	5/16	3/8	7/16	1/2	9/16
12½	Sextile	Shallop	Sharpset	Shelve	Shocking	Shrink
13	Sexton	Shallow	Shastra	Shelving	Shoeblack	Shrinkage
13½	Sextuple	Shallowness	Shatter	Shepherd	Shoemaker	Shrivel
14	Shabbily	Shalote	Shattering	Shepherdess	Shoestring	Shroud
14½	Shabbiness	Sham	Shave	Sherbet	Shook	Shrub
15	Shabby	Shambles	Shaving	Sherd	Shoot	Shrubbery
15½	Shack	Shambling	Shawl	Sheriff	Shooter	Shrug
16	Shackle	Shamed	Shawm	Sherry	Shooting	Shrugged
16½	Shade	Shamefaced	Sheaf	Shield	Shop	Shrunk
17	Shadiness	Shameful	Shearer	Shieldless	Shopman	Shuck
17½	Shadow	Shameless	Sheath	Shift	Shopping	Shudder
18	Shadowed	Shaming	Sheathing	Shifter	Shore	Shuffle
18½	Shady	Shamois	Sheave	Shiftless	Shoreless	Shun
19	Shaft	Shamrock	Shed	Shillaly	Shorten	Shutter
19½	Shagged	Shank	Shedder	Shilling	Shorthand	Shuttle
20	Shagginess	Shanty	Sheeny	Shimmer	Shortly	Sbyness
21	Shagreen	Shape	Sheep	Shine	Shortness	Sibilant
22	Shake	Shapeless	Sheepcot	Shingle	Shorts	Sibyl
23	Shaken	Shaping	Sheepfold	Shining	Shotten	Sicken
24	Shale	Shard	Sheepish	Shipboard	Shoulder	Sickle
25	Shalloon	Share	Sheepskin	Shipmate	Shout	Sickliness
26	. . . . . .	Shark	Sheet	Shipper	Shovel	Sideboard
27	. . . . . .	Sharp	Sheeting	Shipshape	Shoveler	Sidelong
28	. . . . . .	Sharper	Shekel	Shipwreck	Show	Siding
29	. . . . . .	Sharply	Shelf	Shipwright	Shower	Sideral
30	. . . . .	Sharpness	Shell	Shire	Showering	Sidesman
31	. . . .		Shellac	Shirk	Showiness	Sidewalk
32	. . . .		Shellfish	Shirking	Shown	Sideways
33	. . . .		Shelter	Shirred	Shrank	Siesta
34	. . . .		Shelterless	Shirting	Shred	Sift
35	. . . .		Sheltie	Shiver	Shrew	Sifter
36	. . . .			Shivering	Shrewd	Sighted
37	. . . .			Shoad	Shrewdly	Sightless
38	. . . .			Shoal	Shrewdness	Sign
39	. . . .			Shoalless	Shrewish	Signal
40	. . . .			Shock	Shrift	Signalize
41	. . . .				Shrike	Signature
42	. . . .				Shrill	Signet
43	. . . .				Shrillness	Signify
44	. . . .				Shrimp	Silence
45	. . . .				Shrine	Silex

TELEGRAPHIC CODE.

Size of Bolts 5-8 to 1 1-4 Diameter Inclusive, Longer than 15 inches.

	$\frac{5}{8}$	$\frac{3}{4}$	$\frac{7}{8}$	1	$1\frac{1}{8}$	$1\frac{1}{4}$
15½	Silicon	Sinus	Slam	Sliver	Snappish	Socialism
16	Siliqua	Siphon	Slander	Slobber	Snare	Society
16½	Silk	Sipped	Slanderous	Sloop	Snarler	Socinian
17	Silker	Siren	Slang	Sloping	Snatch	Socket
17½	Silkiness	Sirloin	Slant	Sloppy	Snatcher	Socratic
18	Silkworm	Sirup	Slanting	Slothful	Sneak	Soda
18½	Sillabub	Sitter	Slantwise	Slouch	Sneaking	Sodality
19	Silvan	Sitting	Slap	Sloven	Sneer	Soddy
19½	Silver	Situation	Slapdash	Slowness	Sneering	Sodium
20	Silversmith	Siva	Slapjack	Slug	Snicker	Sofa
21	Similar	Sixfold	Slash	Sluggard	Sniff	Soffit
22	Similarity	Sixpence	Slate	Sluice	Snivel	Soften
23	Similitude	Skate	Slater	Slumber	Sniveler	Softly
24	Simmer	Skater	Slattern	Slump	Snob	Softness
25	Simony	Skating	Slave	Slur	Snobbish	Soggy
26	Simoon	Skeleton	Slavery	Slush	Snore	Sojourn
27	Simper	Skewer	Slavish	Slyboots	Snow	Solace
28	Simple	Skid	Slay	Smack	Snowball	Solacement
29	Simpleton	Skiff	Sled	Smallness	Snowdrift	Solar
30	Simplify	Skillet	Sledding	Smartness	Snub	Soldier
31	Simulate	Skillful	Sledge	Smatter	Snuff	Soldierly
32	Simulation	Skimmer	Sleek	Smatterer	Snuffbox	Solecism
33	Sinapism	Skinflint	Sleekness	Smear	Snuffer	Solemn
34	Sincere	Skinner	Sleep	Smelter	Snuffle	Solemness
35	Sincerity	Skipper	Sleepless	Smirk	Snug	Solicitor
36	Sinecure	Skirmish	Sleet	Smiter	Snugly	Solicitude
37	Sinew	Skirt	Sleeve	Smithy	Snugness	Solidly
38	Sinewless	Skittish	Slender	Smoke	Soak	Solidness
39	Sinful	Skittles	Slice	Smoker	Soaker	Solitaire
40	Sinfulness	Skiver	Slide	Smokiness	Soap	Solitude
41	Singe	Skulk	Sliding	Smoldering	Soapstone	Solo
42	Singing	Skull	Slightness	Smoothness	Soapsuds	Solstice
43	Single	Skylark	Slim	Smother	Soar	Soluble
44	Singsong	Skylight	Slimness	Smuggle	Soaring	Solution
45	Singular	Slab	Sling	Snack	Sober	Solvable
46	Sinister	Slabber	Slinger	Snaffle	Soberly	Solve
47	Sink	Slack	Slip	Snag	Soberness	Solvency
48	Sinner	Slacken	Slipknot	Snagged	Sobriety	Solvent
49	Sinuate	Slackness	Slipper	Snail	Sociable	Somber
50	Sinuosity	Slag	Slipshod	Snake	Social	Sombrous

TELEGRAPHIC CODE.

Per one hundred pieces, ... Tabby.
For the lot, ... Table.
Good common Iron, ... Texture.
Guaranteed quality Bridge Iron, ... Thaler.
Soft Steel, 10 to 12 carbon, ... Tharos.
Norway Iron, ... Thatcher.

Dates	Last Month	This Month	Next Month
1	Tracker	Transcribe	Traveler
2	Trackless	Transept	Traversing
3	Tractable	Transfer	Travesty
4	Traction	Transfigure	Trawler
5	Traded	Transfix	Trawlnet
6	Tradeless	Transform	Treachery
7	Trademark	Transfuse	Treadle
8	Tradesman	Transgress	Treason
9	Trading	Transient	Treasury
10	Tradition	Transit	Treatise
11	Traduce	Transition	Treatment
12	Traffic	Transitory	Trellis
13	Trafficker	Translate	Tremble
14	Tragedian	Translation	Tremendous
15	Tragedy	Translucent	Tremolite
16	Tragic	Transmit	Trenchant
17	Tragus	Transmove	Trepanning
18	Trailer	Transom	Trespass
19	Training	Transparent	Triangle
20	Traipse	Transpire	Tribulation
21	Traitor	Transplant	Tribunal
22	Traitress	Transported	Tributary
23	Tramble	Transverse	Trident
24	Tramming	Trapan	Trigger
25	Tramp	Trapdoor	Trillium
26	Tramroad	Trapeze	Trilobite
27	Tramway	Trapezium	Trimmer
28	Tranquil	Trapper	Trinket
29	Transaction	Trappings	Tripod
30	Transaudient	Trashiness	Triton
31	Transcend	Travail	Triumvir

INDEX

INDEX—Continued.

INDEX—Continued.